SCOTLAND

of one hundred years ago

General William Booth (1829–1912) of the Salvation Army, pictured in an open-top automobile at the junction of Gardyne Street and Millgate, at Friockheim [pronounced Freekum], Parish of Kirkden, Angus, 9 September 1904.

Children pose at the ancient Mercat [market] Cross at the twin villages of Kirk Yetholm and Town Yetholm, famous for their gypsy settlements and smuggling Scots whisky across the Border, c. 1890.

SCOTLAND

of one hundred years ago

RAYMOND LAMONT-BROWN

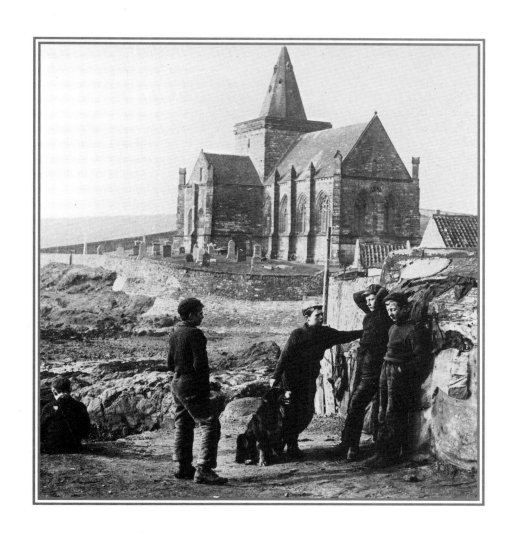

SUTTON PUBLISHING

First published in 1997 by
Sutton Publishing Limited · Phoenix Mill
Thrupp · Stroud · Gloucestershire · GL5 2BU

British Library Cataloguing in Publication Data
A catalogue record for this book is available from the British Library

ISBN 0-7509-1421-1

Half-title photograph: 'Penny farthings' and a large-wheeled tricycle outside the Gordon Arms, Yarrow Valley, near St Mary's Loch, Selkirkshire, c. 1899. The riders wear the uniform of a Cycling Club. (Photo: C.P. Milligan, Dundee)
Title page photograph: Fisher boys at St Monance, Fife, c. 1880. Across the mouth of the St Monance Burn stands the thirteenth-century church, renovated in 1826. (Photo: Alexander Brown Patterson MBE)
Endpapers, front: the 4th Earl of Mansfield with family and friends at Scone Palace; back: children of the Royal School of Dunkeld, Perthshire, playing in the River Tay in 1891.

 ™ ALAN SUTTON™ and SUTTON™ are the
trade marks of Sutton Publishing Limited

Typeset in 11/13pt Bembo Mono.
Typesetting and origination by Sutton Publishing Limited.
Printed in Great Britain by WBC Ltd, Bridgend.

An Edwardian view of the junction of Dock Street and Commercial Street, Dundee; the Navigation School stands to the left.

CONTENTS

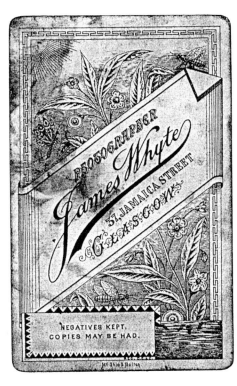

Title-page of W.H. Fox Talbot's first Scottish Album, Sun Pictures in Scotland, *1844.*

Carte-de-visite portrait of a Victorian lady, c. 1870, by photo-artist John Fergus, Largs.

Advertising reverse of a carte-de-visite by James Whyte, 37 Jamaica Street, Glasgow, c. 1870.

THE SCOTTISH WAY
OF PHOTOGRAPHY

Melrose Abbey, Roxburghshire, Heriot's Hospital, and Sir Walter Scott's Monument, Edinburgh, were among the earliest subjects for photographs ever taken in Scotland. They appeared in *Sun Pictures in Scotland*, a limited edition of twenty-three photographic views taken by the English physicist William Henry Fox Talbot (1800–77) – the 'Father of Modern Photography' – who first set up his cameras in Scotland in 1844. It was a volume that was to have a singular place in the history of Scots photography as it was the precursor of a myriad Victorian photo albums. Fox Talbot was an exponent of the calotype photographic process which was fine for capturing landscapes and architecture, but the daguerreotype process – invented by Frenchman Louis Jacques Mandé Daguerre (1789–1851) – was better for portraiture. One Richard Beard controlled copyright of the daguerreotype process in England and Wales, and charged extortionate fees for its licence, so the first daguerreotype studio was opened by a Mr Edwards in Buchanan Street, Glasgow, in 1843. Although expensive at 'a guinea for a portrait', the studio became very popular, the pictures being mounted on card in the French style known as *carte-de-visite*.

There were no patent or copyright restrictions on the calotype process in Scotland either and St Andrews was hailed as the 'Home of the Calotype'. A group of science enthusiasts, including the Principal of the United Colleges of St Salvator and St Leonard, Sir David Brewster (1781–1868), the Medical Officer of Health for St Andrews, Dr John Adamson (1810–70), and Major (Sir) Hugh Lyon Playfair (1786–1861), began experimenting with the calotype process soon after Fox Talbot had shared his knowledge with them. Dr John Adamson is credited with producing the first calotype portrait taken in Scotland. Adamson encouraged his brother Robert (1821–48)

Jedburgh Abbey, 1872, with Jed Water in the foreground. In 1875 the old parish church which had stood in the nave since 1671 was transferred to a new site at the initiative of William Schomberg Robert Kerr, 9th Marquess of Lothian. In 1913 the ruined abbey church was placed in the guardianship of HM Office of Works, the first of the great Border abbeys to pass into state ownership.

to perfect his skills in the calotype process and in 1843 Robert opened a studio at Rock House, Calton Hill, Edinburgh. Sir David Brewster introduced Robert Adamson to the artist David Octavius Hill (1802–70) and together Hill and Adamson produced some of the first photographic portraits ever. Dr Adamson also encouraged his former laboratory assistant Thomas Rodger (1833–83) to study the photographic process, and Rodger set up his own studio at 6 St Mary's Place, St Andrews; sadly, when the studio closed in the early 1900s, many of Rodgers' glass photographic plates were destroyed.

A great boost to the advancement of photography in Scotland began when the daguerreotype and calotype developments were superseded by the wet collodion process invented by Frederick Scott Archer in association with Peter Fry. This made photographic techniques cheaper and the Victorian photographic album became an important part of the Scottish drawing-room, sporting the work of such as James Valentine (1815–80) of Dundee and George Washington Wilson (1823–93) of Aberdeen.

By the late 1850s the technology of photography was well established in Scotland and was energetically promoted as a hobby with the founding of the Photographic Society of Scotland. Sir David Brewster did much to popularise the stereoscopic picture (wherein two identical images are looked at in a 'viewer'), and in 1861 Sir James Clerk Maxwell (1831–79) described the first colour process in photography. But even colour was not unknown in Scotland as hand-coloured daguerreotypes had appeared there in the 1860s.

For Victorian visitors to Scotland bent on making a photographic record of their stay, the process was slow, cumbersome and expensive. For the keen there was a range of craftsman-made wood and metal cameras, and chemists' shops began to sell photographic equipment, ranging from the 1880s actinometers (to calculate exposure times) to the latest folding, bellows dry-plate cameras. The lengthy exposure needed and the porterage of bulky equipment – tripods, glass plates and carrying cases – led to the exposure of half a dozen photographs a day being considered good.

Yet among the lady and gentleman amateurs setting up their equipment were to be seen professional photographers on assignment. One such was Thomas Annan (1829–87), who began his career as a photographic copier of works of art. He is remembered today as a recorder of street life in wynds (narrow lanes) and vennels (alleys) through his commissions from Glasgow's city fathers immortalising their urban renewal programmes. Annan thus elevated the 'social photograph' to a classic level, his images portraying the same distressing social conditions as the novels of his contemporary, Charles Dickens.

Thomas Annan's achievements for the reality pictures of Glasgow, were echoed by men such as Alexander Johnston (b. *c.* 1830) for the countryside. From his studio at Wick, Johnston produced a series of negatives which bring nineteenth-century Scottish history vividly to life. He recorded the everyday work and play of one area, from coopering and sailmaking to boatbuilding and gold mining. Such work encouraged the amateur photographer to be bolder and innovative in subject range.

A revolutionary change for Scotland's keen photographers came with the first Kodak camera in June 1888. Invented by the young American George Eastman, it contained a roll of celluloid film and was simple to use. People who had never contemplated taking up photography were now able to take competent pictures. 'An appropriate wedding present' was the by-line of one camera advert, while an early testimonial gushed: 'It is the greatest boon on earth to the travelling man . . . to be able to bring home, at so small an outlay of time and money, a complete photographic memorandum'. The outlay in the 1880s was around £5 5s for a simple Kodak camera; twenty years before a photographic set would have cost over £40 at a time when families were being raised on 10s per week.

By the time Queen Victoria's reign ended the folding pocket camera had appeared. At the turn of the century too, the Brownie camera became popular with children. At 5s it was an ideal birthday present. As a new generation of young Scots snapped away with their 'Box Brownies', the rich were pursuing a new innovation: in 1893 the Thomas Edison Kinescope made its debut with moving images. Thus Scotland entered a new age of photography.

VICTORIAN & EDWARDIAN SCOTLAND

When Queen Victoria came to the throne just after 2 p.m. on 20 June 1837, after the death of her uncle William IV, there were two quite distinctive Scotlands. For centuries the Highlanders in the north had enjoyed their own culture quite separate from that of the Lowlanders in the south. For centuries they had survived as close-knit, Gaelic-speaking communities loyal to their mostly Tory chiefs and proud of their heritage, sustained by a Roman Catholic or Episcopalian faith. The differences between them had constructed a mutual barrier of animosity.

Centred upon Edinburgh, the Lowlanders were partisan towards England in speech and in trade, and were largely Presbyterian and Whig. As the century progressed Scotland moved further along the road to Anglicisation. The Scots upper classes were educated more and more in English schools and universities, and the country's capital and industries were coming under the control of English boards of directors. In academe the picture was the same, with the professoriate being constantly recruited from England, and the student bodies containing a high proportion of English undergraduates. In 1903, for instance, 54 per cent of the medical students at Edinburgh University were non-Scots.

Families gather for a village picnic at Coldingham Beach, Berwickshire, in 1908. To the centre left stand the beach huts, once an important feature of the strand.

Waggoners unload timber from the Douglas Castle estate, at Douglas Station, Lanarkshire, c. 1898. The castle was demolished between 1938 and 1948.

Queen Victoria died at 6.30 p.m. on 22 January 1901 at Osborne House on the Isle of Wight, and by this time two new Scotlands overlaid the previous ones; the new Scotlands were realigned east–west because of industrialisation and the Hibernianisation of Clydeside. The population too had doubled.

Comparatively inaccessible areas of Scotland still existed one hundred years ago and this factor should not be underestimated in terms of judging national perceptions. Although pioneer railways such as the Dundee to Newtyle line, incorporated as early as 1826, had opened up large tracts of Scotland, the railway network failed to penetrate many parts of the far north and west. Thus a large portion of the Highlands remained unvisited and unrecorded by Victorian and Edwardian photographers.

Yet transport was to bring enormous changes for Scotland between 1837 and 1910. In 1837 the horse still reigned supreme, and four-wheeled wagons and two-wheeled carts, all with iron-rimmed wheels, were the most common methods of road haulage. The sight of horses yoked to ploughs and leisurely cutting straight furrows was one that attracted little attention in Scotland and every farm worker was expected to know the basics of horse care. Even in the smallest parish the smithy regularly shod one hundred pairs of horses. The development of the steam engine and petrol-driven traction, however, mirrored the steady decline of the horse, and compounded with industrialisation the change of Scotland's homebase from a rural setting to a town-centred one.

Scotland's Victorian and Edwardian cities evolved on the new economic bases set out in the eighteenth century with the growth in population and the expansion of industry. As they grew in size a sprawling expansion took place at the outskirts; and as the population began to ebb away from the city centres, so it began to flood into the neighbouring villages and towns, and large rural areas were taken over by suburbia. Houses in the city centres, the medieval core of Scotland's larger thoroughfares, began to be pulled down and replaced by shops, banks, warehouses, factories and offices, and by the 1880s and 1890s the large city centres had been redesigned and the new layouts were to last for sixty years. From the early years of Victoria's reign then, undeveloped land around Scottish cities was formed into suburbia to make new 'superior' properties for the rich and 'industrial' properties for the working class.

Glasgow was to evolve as the real Victorian city in Scotland, with a strongly growing population within its boundaries. Nowhere else in Britain was there such a concentrated city population than in Glasgow. The city responded by changing from a commercial to an industrial base, and as the decades passed the city adapted to new opportunities to generate huge civic enterprise. By 1891 some 19.5 per cent of the country's 4.5 million population lived in Glasgow. And by the mid-years of Victoria's reign a keen rivalry had developed between Glasgow and Edinburgh, illustrated by the familiar jingle 'Edinburgh is the capital, Glasgow has the capital'.

Tom Bolton, postman at Reston Station, Berwickshire, c. 1910. Reston was an important junction on the East Coast Railway (North British Railway, Edinburgh–Berwick, 1844) linking hill and country villages to the developing communications system.

View of North Street, St Andrews, Fife, looking towards St Salvator's College and Chapel (1450–60), c. 1908. Next to Beethoven Lodge (centre right) stands a now vanished vernacular fore-stair cottage. At far left is the tower of Martyrs' Church which was built in 1843 and modified in 1852.

A quartet of officers of the Atholl Highlanders [the private army of the Duke of Atholl] outside the front entrance of Blair Castle, c. 1899. Second from the left is John, 7th Duke of Atholl (d. 1917).

The doyen of Victorian philanthropists, John Patrick Crichton-Stuart, 3rd Marquis of Bute (1847–1900). He was a keen restorer of ancient monuments.

Other areas of Scotland polarised into specific interests as Victoria's reign developed. For instance, the Firth of Clyde developed a wide range of resorts. Golf flourished at St Andrews, Prestwick, Musselburgh, Turnberry and Troon, while the east coast of Scotland from Eyemouth to the Moray Firth coast was renowned for its herring trade.

By the end of the nineteenth century a huge change had taken place in land proprietorship in Scotland, with family estates of long pedigree passing into the hands of rich merchants, bankers, iron-masters and manufacturers of all kinds. From time to time the aristocratic landowners came out of their hereditary fastnesses to cut an eccentric dash at public gatherings. One such was the 2nd Marquess and 5th Earl of Breadalbane (1796–1862), of Taymouth Castle, who made such an impression at Queen Victoria's Gathering of Highland Volunteers at Edinburgh in 1860 that – as one commentator said – 'one's thoughts travelled back to the days of Prince Charles [Edward Stuart]', for 'there had been no such mustering of warlike men straight from the Highland glens' for a century. The new lairds, who now appeared at

court, on magistrates' benches and on town councils, were able to improve the ancient estates and houses, bought from the old poverty-stricken hereditary owners, and took prominent parts in arts and culture, engendering a new public spirit and philanthropy in churches, schools and villages. Thus a new class developed, particularly in the west of Scotland, where wealthy coal and iron-masters emerged from humble beginnings as working miners.

Scotland also retained throughout the nineteenth century its own calendar of festivals and markets, and from the first minutes of the New Year being summoned in by the bells of Kirk and Tollbooth, Scotland settled down to an annual pattern of life which had been formed by centuries of folklore. Thus in seasonal spirit was Scotland still affected by the old Celtic festivals of Samhuinn (Hallowmass, 1 November), Imbolc (St Bride's Day, February), Beltane (May Day), and Lugnassad (Lammas, August) with their superstitions and customs, all of which gave Scotland's rural life a distinctive flavour. In nineteenth-century Scotland, of course, Christmas was not a holiday and – despite the festival having been given a great

Representing an increasingly mobile population with the advent of cheaper public transport, crowds gather for Sports Day at Wilton Lodge Park, Hawick.

boost in England by both Charles Dickens and Prince Albert – the Scots preferred to celebrate the beginning of the New Year, which they dubbed Hogmanay.

Just as Victorian and Edwardian Scotland still retained the old Scots style of law and education (making it quite different from England), the paying of bills and the hiring of staff, the selling of local goods (sometimes with an individual age-old set of weights and measures) and the feuing (renting) of property was undertaken at the Scottish Quarter Days of Candlemas (2 February), Whitsun (15 May), Lammas (1 August) and Martinmas (11 November).

Nineteenth-century visitors to Scotland always wondered why so much whisky was consumed by the natives. One reason often suggested was the inclemency of the weather, but social historians aver that it was the common man's anaesthetic against the miseries of life at coal-face, iron-forge and quarry. By Victorian times several inns in Scotland still sold an (often home-brewed) raw-grain spirit, adulterated with water but exceedingly potent. The Act of 1823 encouraged many of the illicit stills to become open and thus was laid the foundation of the modern Scotch whisky industry, which was given international scope by the invention of the 'patent still' in 1830 by Aeneas Coffey.

Visitors remarked how whisky seemed to have little effect on such as the Highland gillies who organised their shooting parties, nevertheless the social ills of drunkenness were to be sorely felt in Scots culture a hundred years ago. Yet the nineteenth century also saw the spawning of a multitude of temperance societies, anti-smoking leagues and the expansion of public philanthropy through private funds.

The beginning of Queen Victoria's reign had been a historical watershed for Scotland and the accession of her son Edward was to mark another. Rich and poor Scots alike looked to Edward VII's monarchy with great optimism. Their new sovereign was to give them public splendour and his colourful, avuncular affability charmed everyone after his mother's largely stiff grey court. Scots youth looked for the Edwardian Age to strip away what they saw as the false morality of religion, hypocritical social behaviour and the hollow ideas of Victorian philosophy. When Edward VII died at Buckingham Palace on 6 May 1910 he was seen to have given them ordered, prosperous and sunny days during his reign and they looked forward with hope and confidence. Four years into the reign of the new king George V, Scotland's ebullient youth was to be slaughtered as never before in the mud along the Franco-Belgian border.

Chapter 1

PORTRAIT OF A PHOTOGRAPHER

*I*n terms of the history of photography in Scotland, John Wood put the village of Coldingham and the south-east borderland of Berwickshire firmly on the map. John had been born in humble circumstances at Old Scarlaw Farm, Longformacus, Berwickshire, in 1854, the son of William Wood, a shepherd.

Mid-Victorian rural-coastal Scotland offered little in the way of employment for the young male outside agriculture and the white fish trade, so John Wood went to Glasgow in 1872 to take up apprenticeship as a joiner. In 1877 he married Rosina Lynch and set up home in Glasgow as a journeyman-joiner. It seems that the marriage turned sour and the relationship ended in divorce. Wood returned to Berwickshire to live at Coldingham, and in the parlance of local gossip, 'took up with' a village widow, Margaret Kerr, whom he married in 1890.

By this time Wood had set himself up as a photographer, as his marriage certificate testifies. He had been living in Glasgow at the time when studio photographic portraiture was all the rage and the new fashion for collecting albums of photographs and postcards of Scottish landscapes and townscapes was beginning to develop. It is likely that in this atmosphere John Wood became interested in photography as a career. It is not known if he actually undertook a photographic course, but it is probable that he was self-taught.

Wood set up a studio at Coldingham which was to be his home for two decades. His wife died in 1911 aged 59, and Wood himself died on 4 August 1914 and was interred in an unmarked

Photographer John Wood (1854–1914), of Coldingham, Berwickshire, 1890. He carries a leather photographic glass-slide case of the period. Right: Margaret Wood (1852–1911), his wife, with twins Margaret and Agnes, 1890. Wood's prints depict an interesting range of working-class clothing.

Red-pantiled cottage with lean-to shed and twin water-butts at Fishers Brae, Coldingham, c. 1900. The perambulator is of the style of the 1890s.

Workmen prepare to re-harl Lindens, High Street, Coldingham, c. 1908. Such weatherproof roughcasting was popular in Victorian and Edwardian Scotland.

The road to St Abbs harbour village from Coldingham, c. 1910. The clothes look like 'Sunday Best' outfits.

A drayman stops outside David Ewart's Anchor Inn, the Square, Coldingham, c. 1910.

grave in Coldingham Priory churchyard. Wood's extant photographs remain a remarkable collection not only because of their quality and the manner of their preservation, but also their content: they depict a society long gone and village scenes that are barely recognisable today.

Local tradition has it that Wood's photographic plates were disposed of by his daughter Evelyn in a piecemeal fashion. Some were apparently used to glaze greenhouses and for other mundane purposes, but about six hundred survived at a market garden; having been rediscovered in 1983, they were preserved and now form the centrepiece of the John Wood Collection in a museum at Coldingham established by the Thomson family.

The Scottish border counties spawned a number of other talented photographers. Mention should be made of the brothers J. and R. Clapperton who set up studios at Galashiels, Berwickshire, and Selkirk, Selkirkshire, in 1867. R. Clapperton's studio was to survive for 120 years and reflected all the changing fashions of photography. In fact the work of the border photographers was to be collected by the highest in the land.

Stonemasons pause in their work on Robertson Memorial Hall, still extant at Coldingham.

THE EFFICACY OF BLACK SLUGS AT COLDINGHAM

A story, the parallel in some respects of 'Bessie Bell and Mary Grey,' is applicable to Allanhaugh Peel, to which two young maidens retired 'during a famine and fended themselves on oat-meal and a barrel of snails; and it is further said that on this diet they had thriven very well, and were fair and plump, while all around were almost famished.'

The snail myth is not confined to Teviotdale. It is told of two old women at Coldingham, that in a period of distress they had kept themselves alive by means of a barrel of black slugs which they had salted. 'Slugs and snails were anciently, and are to this day, a popular remedy in consumptive complaints.'

History of the Berwickshire Naturalists' Club, 1887

COLDINGHAM RHYMES

The Lovely Girls of Coldingham

The shore for *cuddies* and *buddies*	[donkeys/folk]
Northfield for *clashes* and *lees*,	[gossip/lies]
Couldingham for bonnie young lassies	
Hymooth for *randies* and thieves.	[Eyemouth/beggars]

The Mean Girl of Press Castle

We'll hunt the *Pootie* through the Press,	[mean one]
We'll hunt the Pootie through and through	
We'll hunt the Pootie through the Press,	
Her beauty we'll pursue.	
She has a lad in Coudingham,	
Anither in the Law	[another]
But the bonniest lad amang them a'	
Is the *stewart* o' *Purris Ha'*.	[steward/Purvis Hall]

Chapter 2

QUEEN VICTORIA'S ROYAL HOUSEHOLD IN SCOTLAND

*W*hen Queen Victoria came to the throne in 1837 members of the royal family were strangers in Scottish society. Except for a fleeting visit by King George IV in 1822, no reigning monarch had travelled north of the border since Charles I. Yet Victoria inherited as Queen the ceremonial Royal Household of courtiers in Scotland, which largely consisted of elderly, aristocratic, hereditary landowners. The New Edinburgh Almanac of 1838 lists them under the leadership of five officers of the crown.

The hereditary grand constable and knight marischal was William George Hay, Earl of Erroll, of Slains Castle, Aberdeenshire. The hereditary royal standard-bearer was H. Scrymgeour Wedderburn of Birkhall. The hereditary standard-bearer was James Maitland, Earl of Lauderdale, of Thirlestane Castle, Berwickshire. The lord president of the court of session and lord justice-general for Scotland was the Rt Hon. Charles Hope, and the vice-admiral for Scotland was William Schaw Cathcart, Viscount Cathcart, of Cathcart Castle, Renfrew.

Victoria also had seven officers of state in Scotland and their deputies; they included the keeper of the great seal, George William Campbell, Duke of Argyll, and the lord privy seal, Robert Saunders Dundas, Viscount Melville. There were also twenty-nine assorted Scottish Household courtiers, each with a court title ranging from

Queen Victoria in a pose typical of her widowed years, c. 1870. Such photographs were given to Scottish courtiers as keepsakes.

HIGHLAND DRESS

Black silk velvet Full Dress DOUBLET. Silk lined.
Set of silver CELTIC or CREST BUTTONS for Doublet
Superfine Tartan Full Dress KILT.
Short TREWS.
Full Dress Tartan STOCKINGS.
Full Dress long SHOULDER PLAID.
Full dress white hair SPORRAN – silver mounted and Tassels.
Patent leather and silver chain STRAP for SPORRAN.
Full Dress silver mounted DIRK with Knife and Fork.
Full Dress silver mounted SKEAN DHU with Knife.
Patent leather SHOULDER BELT, silver mounted.
Patent leather WAIST BELT, silver clasp.
Silver mounted SHOULDER BROOCH.
Silver KILT PIN.
Lace JABOT.
One pair BUCKLES for instep of SHOES.
One pair small ankle BUCKLES for SHOES.
Full Dress BROGUES.
Highland CLAYMORE.
Glengarry or Balmoral, CREST or ORNAMENT.

Dress Worn at Court (Guide)

'bread and biscuit baker' to 'limner' (painter), and from 'falconer' to 'historiographer'; all came under the hereditary master of the household, the Duke of Argyll.

In addition there were the deans and chaplains of the Chapel Royal, and the hereditary keepers of the royal palaces of Holyroodhouse, Falkland, Scone, Linlithgow and Lochmaben, and the palace-castles of Rothesay, Dunstaffnage, Dunoon and Carrick.

These then, formed Victoria's ceremonial court. During her first visit to Scotland in 1842, she fell in love with the country; after she and Prince Albert had purchased the estate and castle of Balmoral in 1852 a new domestic court was established. Among her permanent household staff at Balmoral were a number of eccentric characters, including John Brown, her loyal gillie of thirty-four years' service, and Dr Alexander Profeit, the lesser-known 'Commissioner on Deeside' (i.e., head of the domestic household).

Queen Victoria (1819–1901) and her consort Prince Albert (1819–61), whom she had married in 1841, pictured around 1857.

Prince Albert Edward (1841–1910), Prince of Wales, always a reluctant visitor to his mother's Scottish court, pictured around 1857.

Most courtiers dreaded the tedious two-day, twice-yearly journey from Windsor to Balmoral, while the restrictive rules the Queen set out concerning conduct at Balmoral were tersely described by courtiers as 'balmorality'. None was more resistant to travel to the Scottish court than Prince Albert Edward, Prince of Wales, who was dragged unwillingly from his pursuit of pleasure in London. Yet the later years of his own life were to be brightened by the attentions of a Scottish landowner's daughter.

QUEEN VICTORIA'S JOURNAL

BALMORAL, October 14th, 1867
GEN. GREY ASKED TO SEE ME when I came in, and said he was sorry to alarm me, but must show me a telegram from Mr. Hardy, reporting that the Mayor of Manchester [*a statue of the Prince Consort, the gift of the Queen, was to be unveiled there by HM*] had informed him, having the news from a reliable source, that the Fenians had said they meant to try and seize me here, and were starting to-day or to-morrow! Too foolish!! Mr. Hardy added that special precautions should be taken, so Gen. Grey asked to be allowed to send at once for a detachment of troops from Aberdeen to be placed at Abergeldie, but letting it appear as if it were for to-morrow's ceremony. He has also asked for additional police.

BALMORAL, November 22nd, 1871
BREAKFASTED FOR THE FIRST TIME AGAIN with my children, and felt it was a step forward and I was returning to ordinary life. Heard dear Bertie had 'mild typhoid fever' and I at once determined to send off Sir William Jenner to Sandringham. This was gratefully accepted by Alix. Felt very anxious. This fearful fever, and at this very time of the year! Everyone much distressed.

BALMORAL, June 19th, 1879
AFTER DINNER LEILA ERROLL READ, and I was writing, when, just before 11, a telegram was given me with the message that it contained bad news. When I, in alarm, asked what, I was told it was that the Prince Imperial [*of France*] had been killed. I feel a thrill of horror in even writing it. I kept on saying 'No, no, it can't be!' To die in such an awful way is too shocking! Poor dear Empress! her only child, her *all*, gone! I am really in despair. He was such an amiable, good young man, who would have made such a good Emperor for France one day. It is a real misfortune. The more one thinks of it the worse it becomes. Got to bed very late, it was just dawning! and little sleep did I get.

BALMORAL, June 20th, 1886
HAVE ENTERED THE 50TH YEAR OF MY REIGN and my Jubilee year . . . All my ladies and gentlemen sent me a

Prince of Wales's visit to Dupplin Castle, near Forteviot, Perthshire, the home of the Earl and Countess of Kinnoull, August 1870. The Prince of Wales stands far left, with his three-year-old daughter Princess Louise; the Princess of Wales (in white) leans on the pillar (left) with her sons Prince Albert Victor and Prince George. Their host stands in the centre reading.

Visit of HRH Prince George, Duke of York, to Keith Hall, Inverurie, Aberdeenshire, the home of the Earl and Countess of Kintore, 26 July 1894. His hostess stands next to him (with umbrella).

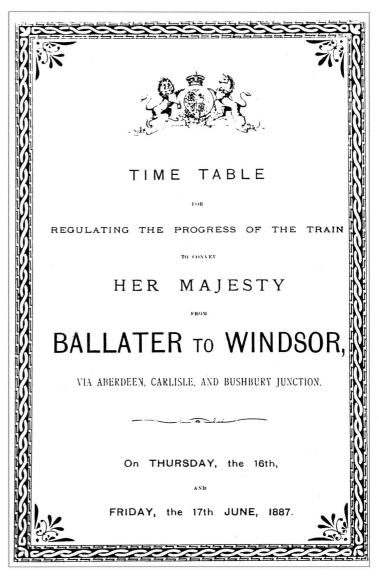

beautiful large basket of flowers, which touched me very much. Of course the real celebration is only to be next year, when the fifty years are completed. Quantities of people have telegraphed to me.

BALMORAL, June 20th, 1896
FIFTY-NINE YEARS SINCE I CAME TO THE THRONE! What a long time to bear so heavy a burden! God has guided me in the midst of terrible trials, sorrows, and anxieties, and has wonderfully protected me. I have lived to see my dear country and vast Empire prosper and expand, and be wonderfully loyal! Received many kind telegrams.

Queen Victoria's Journals, ed. G.E. Buckle, 1926–32

CHILDHOOD HOME OF THE KING'S MISTRESS

Mrs Alice Frederica Keppel, daughter of Admiral Sir William Edmonstone and his wife Mary Elizabeth, spent many of her childhood years at Duntreath Castle. The castle lies in Strathblane on the level land at the bottom of the Blane Valley, about 1½ miles north-west of Blanefield in Stirlingshire. Developed from the core of a tower-house built after 1452, the castle became a Victorian mansion and during 1888–9 Alice's brother Archie, who inherited the baronetcy, greatly renovated and expanded it into a sumptuous home.

In later life Alice's daughter Sonia recalled Duntreath in her mother's day:

Duntreath was a square castle built round a courtyard, strengthened at each corner by four pepperpot towers. Twin arches governed the approach to the courtyard, punctured by twin doors of admittance. Each side of the house had a separate entity, but the arches welded the two sides together, like clasps of a box . . . One of the doors was the front door which led into a long low, panelled hall, filled with beautiful plants . . . The pervading smell of tuberoses was delicious.

Edwardian Daughter, 1958

The Edmonstone family belonged to the upper-class society which functioned on a national rather than a local level. Alice's father, who was an admiral, and a naval aide-de-camp to Queen Victoria, moved in Court circles; when Alice was five her father was elected Conservative MP for Stirlingshire.

As the proprietor of a Scottish country estate, Admiral Edmonstone enjoyed a privileged but rather onerous position. In contrast to English squires, he was not treated with deference, but was regarded in the Scottish way as a father figure and custodian of his estate.

Alice's childhood was typical of that in any Victorian upper-class family, training her for her future role in wealthy society; as a girl, she received only a 'once-over-lightly' education. Stifled by the schoolroom at Duntreath Castle, Alice spent much time with the estate and domestic staff; her influence can still be seen in the design of the rock gardens and waterfalls outside the castle.

Royal visit to Duntreath, September 1909. King Edward VII sits in the centre with Alice Keppel's daughter Sonia by his left knee; her elder daughter Violet sits on the extreme right. George Keppel stands first left (with dog) and Alice fourth from the right next to the King's equerry Col. Hon. Harry Legge.

In 1891 Alice married the Hon. George Keppel, a son of the 7th Earl of Albemarle, and they became established as one of the six hundred or so households then dominating polite society. But by 1893 Alice had taken her first lover; Ernest William Beckett, the future Baron Grimthorpe, was rumoured to have been the father of her elder daughter Violet (who achieved notoriety in her own right as the lover of the writer Vita Sackville West). Five years later Alice met the Prince of Wales: she became and remained his mistress until his death in 1910. When Alice's second daughter Sonia was born rumour suggested that she had a royal father. The visit of her royal lover to her Scottish childhood home in 1909 caused considerable stir among the local people.

STRATHBLANE

Visit of the King to Duntreath Castle

The loyal folks in the little villages of Strathblane and Blanefield were all agog last week over the prospective visit of the King to their beautiful strath. Although the visit was a private one, the inhabitants of the villages and the residents in the surrounding districts were looking forward with keen anticipation to his arrival, and a reception of loyal warmth was assured. The lively interest manifested in the coming of His Majesty, and the pleasure evinced in the expected opportunity of again seeing him in the beautiful strath of the Blane, are mingled with satisfaction that one who is so popular in the district as Sir Archibald Edmonstone was being so highly honoured. For the previous few days the villagers had been busying themselves in preparations. The natural beauties of the strath are such that no adventitious aids are required, but in their own way the villagers showed their loyalty by hanging out their banners and flags on the outer walls. At Blanefield Station a fine floral decorative scheme was carried out by Messrs J. & R. Thyme, Glasgow. Ordinarily it is one of the most attractively set out village stations on the North British system. Mr Shanks, the stationmaster, is a horticulturist of note. The platform was a veritable bower of flowers of many hues and sweetest colours. A prominent feature was the decoration of a pedestal on the island platform at which the Royal train arrived. The pedestal was clothed with evergreens, surmounted by a crown worked out in choice flowers. This decoration was the design of Mr Forsyth, the driver of the local train to Aberfoyle, who had the distinction of driving the Royal train on Saturday

Front façade of Duntreath Castle, c. 1900.

The Library, Duntreath Castle, c. 1900.

The boudoir established by Alice Keppel's mother at Duntreath Castle, c. 1900.

from Lenzie to Blanefield. For the convenience of His Majesty a special gangway was constructed across the line to the entrance of Duntreath. The gangway was arched with evergreens, and at the end was the word 'Welcome', worked in white asters. Another effective floral device was in the form of a crown of red, white, and blue flowers, designed by Mrs Maclennan of Ardoch. At the entrance to Duntreath was a beautiful archway of purple heather, erected under the supervision of M. Horsbrugh the factor in the estate. From all directions crowds poured into Blanefield. They came by train and motors, in carriages, and on cycles. The barricades around the station were densely packed. The pilot engine passed through the station a few minutes before the Royal train, which glided into the platform at half-past 5 o'clock. Sir Archibald Edmonstone and the Duke of Montrose awaited the arrival of the King. On stepping from the Royal compartment, His Majesty shook hands cordially with Sir Archibald and the Duke of Montrose, who conducted him and his equerry, Colonel Legge, to a motor car. King Edward looked the picture of health. He was dressed in a dark suit, with dark grey overcoat and a light brown bowler hat. As he briskly stepped across the gangway loud cheers were raised. The King smiled graciously and repeatedly raised his hat in acknowledgement. The car with His Majesty, his equerry, and his host speedily disappeared along the avenue to the Castle. Following in the second car were the Hon. Mrs Greville, the Hon. Mrs George Keppel, and Lady Sarah Wilson, who journeyed with the train, and in a third car were the Duke of Montrose and Master Edmonstone. The house party at Duntreath included Lord and Lady Brougham, Earl and Countess of Stradbroke, Lady Sarah Wilson, Mrs Leopold de Rothschild, Hon. Mrs Ronald Greville, Hon. Geo. and Mrs Keppel, Sir Thomas Dick Lauder, Lord Elphinstone, Colonel Sir Arthur Davidson, and Colonel H. Legge. During the evening King Edward enjoyed a stroll in the beautiful grounds of the Castle.

This was not the King's first visit to Duntreath. Almost exactly ten years ago – when he was Prince of Wales – he paid a short visit to Duntreath, and expressed himself as greatly charmed with the beauty of the surrounding country and the privacy of Sir Archibald's domain.

On Sunday Strathblane was the Mecca of all sightseers. In anticipation of His Majesty attending the Parish Church service, and favoured with the best of weather, visitors began to pour into the village close by the church as early as 10 o'clock, and commenced to take up favourable positions at the gates of the beautiful little cemetery in which the church is situated. Excellent arrangements had been made previous to Sunday for the orderly accommodation of members of the church, parishioners, and visitors, both inside and outside, and under the charge of Chief-Constable Middleton, the officials and church officers accomplished their trying work in a satisfactory manner. After the space immediately in front of the gates had been filled to its utmost capacity, the people crowded into the large field opposite, which, by nature of its formation, was used as a most convenient grandstand. Then the roadway on either side got lined four and five deep for about a quarter of a mile from the church gates, and also on the walls were hundreds of eager spectators. By half-past 11 o'clock, at which time the gates were opened, it was estimated that there were about five thousand people in the vicinity of the church alone. Ten minutes after the gates were opened the church was completely filled in every part except the gallery, which was reserved for the Royal party. A few visitors had the great fortune to get a seat after all the members and parishioners were accommodated. It still wanted a quarter of an hour to the time of the King's expected arrival when the bell began to ring, and when it had ceased, at about three minutes to 12, loud and prolonged cheering outside heralded the approach of the Royal motor car.

The school children, who had a holiday in honour of the occasion, assembled in the school, and marched by Parklea to the Railway Station. Mr M.F. Chisholm, the schoolmaster, was in charge of the arrangements. Most of the little ones carried flags and banners, and they formed a picturesque procession. Along with the school children ranged up at the station were the members of the local company of the Boy Scouts. They were all in regulation uniform, under Scoutmaster Fraser. His Majesty, on leaving the motor car in company with his host, Sir Archibald Edmonstone, walked across to the little company of Boy Scouts, who formed the guard of honour. His Majesty held a brief conversation with Scoutmaster Fraser, who was in charge of the boys. His Majesty asked the ages of the boys, and Mr Fraser replied that they ranged from 10 to 16 years. 'What do you instruct them in?' was His Majesty's next query. Mr Fraser informed the King of the work the boys did, and His Majesty then remarked – 'I see you are an old soldier yourself. What regiment were you in?' On hearing that it was the Queen's Own Cameron Highlanders, the King remarked, 'Oh, that was my mother's own regiment.' After complimenting the Scoutmaster on the excellent appearance presented by the boys, His Majesty shook hands with him, and left, remarking that he hoped he would continue to be successful. His Majesty, who was dressed in a light grey check jacket suit, with brown boots, brown Hombourg hat, and red tie, had a crimson carnation in his buttonhole. Before entering the train he conversed with Sir Archibald Edmonstone, who presented to him Mr Horsbrugh, his factor, and afterwards the King spoke for several minutes to Mr A.F. Yarrow, the well-known shipbuilder, who has a residence, Campsie Dene, in Blanefield. He also held a conversation with the Hon. George Keppel at the door of the Royal compartment. He bade goodbye to his friends on the platform, including the Edmonstone boys and Miss Violet Keppel. His Majesty then took his place in the Royal saloon. The train was due to leave at 1.50, and glided out of the station amidst ringing cheers two minutes before scheduled time.

Stirling Saturday Observer (18 September 1909)

Chapter 3

THE TRAVELLING CAMERA

S ir John Lubbock (1834–1913), the Victorian banker and scientist and MP for Maidstone, is famous for having secured the passage of the Bank Holidays Act in parliament in 1871. This Act laid down New Year's Day, Christmas Day, Good Friday and the first Mondays of May and August as Bank Holidays in Scotland, and it was to change the whole aspect of mass tourism and travel in Scotland.

The annual holiday became an indispensable part of routine middle-class life in Scotland. As the years passed sea-bathing became increasingly popular and Scots resorts began to offer wheeled bathing machines in which people dressed decorously in their all-enveloping bathing costumes and were trundled down to the water's edge where they emerged discreetly to paddle and bathe.

Scotland had all the scenery – wild heathlands, misty lochs and mountains, ruined castles – essential to the romantic temperament of the early Victorians. Holidays led to an increased interest in 'Nature', promoted by such bodies as The Commons, Open Spaces and Footpaths Preservation Society, founded in 1865. Those who had been brought up in the country, especially those who had been forced to move to towns to find work, developed a new compulsion to discover the flora and fauna of their native

land. Schools also encouraged an interest in nature, teaching children to look for the plants and animals pictured in their textbooks.

One man who did a great deal to facilitate the development of the Scottish tourist trade in an administrative sense was Thomas Cook (1808–92). A woodturner-cum-Baptist missionary, he saw the development of the excursion as a way of directing human endeavour against sloth and sinful self-indulgences; he began to act as a tourist agent, with his first excursion in 1841. In 1846 some 350 trippers set off with Cook on a one guinea excursion from Leicestershire to Edinburgh. At the time there was no railway across the border, so Cook arranged for the group to travel by rail to Fleetwood and thence by steamer to Ardrossan; the journey was completed by rail to Glasgow and Edinburgh. The excursion proved such a novelty that special receptions were held for the travellers at Glasgow and Edinburgh, with bands meeting the party on the platforms and cannon firing in their honour.

Holidays were not only for families in Scotland. The popularity of university extension schemes for non-vocational groups meant that 'reading' and 'photographic' parties, under the tutorship of an academic, regularly set off into the Highlands, islands and

W. Forrest's engraving of Sam Bough's picture of Balmoral Castle from the north, following the renovations to estate and buildings of 1859–60. Royal Deeside, as the local area was to become, was an early target for the burgeoning Victorian tourist trade.

RAILWAY MAP OF SCOTLAND

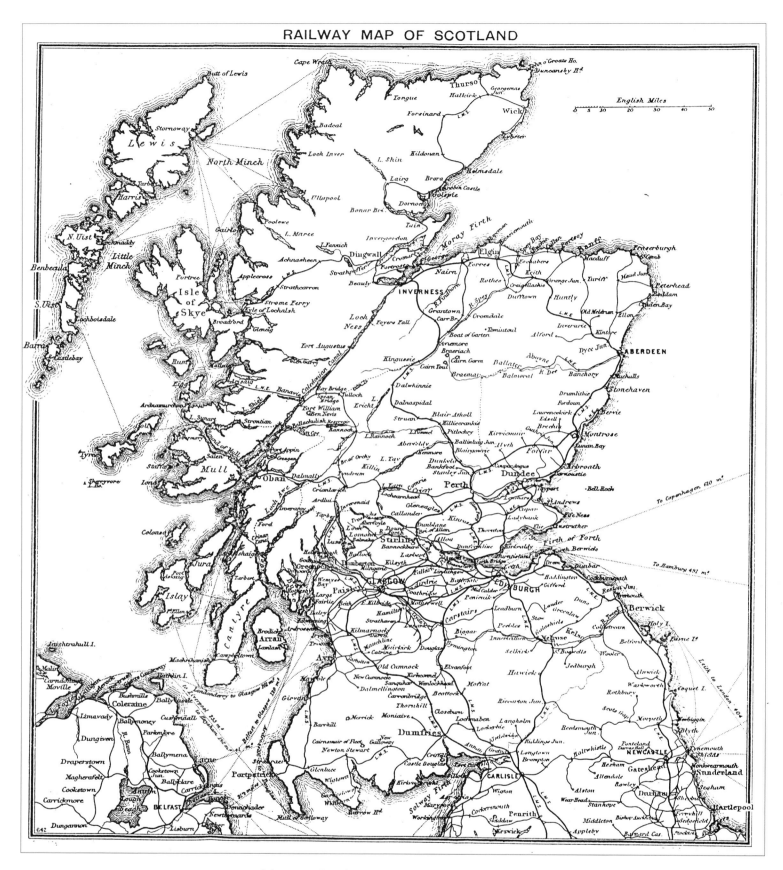

Map of the Scottish railway system as it had developed by 1910.

Thomas Allom's 'The Gathering of the Clans' (1859) at Dunstaffnage Castle and the entrance to Loch Etive. Engravings such as these in the published novels of Sir Walter Scott, encouraged the Victorian traveller to seek out the romantic scenes of Scottish history.

countryside. The trade in published guides also escalated. The early guides to Scotland assumed that travellers would wish to inspect not only ruined abbeys and stately homes, but also breweries, distilleries, foundries and a range of industrial sites. Thus the Scottish holiday developed from its initial role as restorative therapy for the wealthy into a way for everyone to enjoy and record in diaries and photographics, the beauties of the countryside.

THAT D—D WALTER SCOTT!

No more remarkable contrast between the present tourist traffic in this lake region and that of the early part of last century could be supplied than that which is revealed by an incident recorded as having occurred about the year 1814, four years after the publication of Scott's *Lady of the Lake*. An old Highlander, who was met on the top of Ben Lomond, said he had been a guide from the north side of the mountain for upwards of forty years; 'but that d—d Walter Scott, that everybody makes such a work about!' exclaimed he with

vehemence – 'I wish I had him to ferry over Loch Lomond: I should be after sinking the boat, if I drowned myself into the bargain; for ever since he wrote his *Lady of the Lake*, as they call it, everybody goes to see that filthy hole Loch Katrine, then comes round by Luss, and I have had only two gentlemen to guide all this blessed season, which is now at an end. I shall never see the top of Ben Lomond again! – The devil confound his ladies and his lakes, say I!'

If this indignant mountaineer could revisit his early haunts, his grandchildren would have a very different story to tell him of the poet's influence. For one visitor to his beloved mountain in his day there must now be at least a hundred, almost all of whom have had their first longing to see that region kindled by the poems and tales of Scott. No man ever did so much to make his country known and attractive as the Author of *Waverley* has done for Scotland. His fictitious characters have become historical personages in the eyes of the thousands of pilgrims who every year visit the scenes he has described.

Sir Archibald Geikie, *Scottish Reminiscences* (1904)

Harp of the North, farewell! The hills grow dark,
    On purple peaks a deeper shade descending;
In twilight copse the glow-worm lights her spark,
    The deer, half seen, are to the covert wending,
Resume thy wizard elm! the fountain lending,
    And the wild breeze, thy wilder minstrelsy;
Thy numbers sweet with nature's vespers blending,
    With distant echo from the fold and lea,
And herd-boy's evening pipe and hum of housing bee.

Yet, once again farewell, thou Minstrel harp!
    Yet once again, forgive my feeble sway,
And little reck I of the censure sharp
    May idly cavil at an idle lay.
Much have I owed thy strains on life's long way,
    Through secret woes the world has never known,
When on the weary night dawn'd wearier day,
    And bitterer was the grief devour'd alone.
That I o'erlive such woes, Enchantress! is thine own.

Hark! as my lingering footsteps slow retire,
    Some Spirit of the Air has waked thy string!
'Tis now a seraph bold, with touch of fire,
    'Tis now the brush of Fairy's frolic wing.
Receding now, the dying numbers ring
    Fainter and fainter down the rugged dell,
And now the mountain breezes scarcely bring
    A wandering witch-note of the distant spell −
And now, 'tis silent all! − Enchantress, fare thee well!

Sir Walter Scott, *The Lady of the Lake* (1810)

ROWING IN THE HIGHLANDS

Steamboats had not yet been introduced upon the large freshwater lakes of Scotland, except upon Loch Lomond, when I visited the Trossachs region for the first time in 1843. I was rowed the whole length of Loch Katrine in a boat by four stout Highlanders, who sang Gaelic songs, to the cadence of which they kept time with their oars. It was my first entry into the Highlands, and could not have been more impressive. The sun was almost setting as the boat pushed off from Stronachlachar and all the glories of the western sky were cast upon the surrounding girdle of mountains, the reflections of which fell unbroken on the mirror-like surface of the water. As we advanced and the sunset tints died away, the full autumn moon rose above the crest of Ben Venue, and touched off the higher crags with light, while the shadows gathered in deepening black along the lower slopes and the margin of the water. Before we reached the lower end of the lake the silvery sheen filled all the pass of the Trossachs above the sombre forest. The forms of the hills, the changing lights in the sky, and the weird tunes of the boatmen combined to leave on my memory a picture as vivid now as when it was impressed sixty years ago.

Sir Archibald Geikie

MELROSE ABBEY

MELROSE ABBEY,

WITH

Notes Descriptive and Historical.

JOHN HOOD,
Custodian of the Abbey.

TWENTY-FOURTH EDITION.

EDINBURGH
WILLIAM RITCHIE & SONS, LTD., ELDER ST.
1905.

Owned by Anne, Duchess of Buccleuch in Victorian times, Melrose Abbey was given by one of her descendants to HM Office of Works in 1919. John Hood's guide to the abbey was one of the earliest guides published in Scotland.

WHEN TO VIEW THE ABBEY

If thou would'st view fair Melrose aright,
Go visit it by the pale moonlight;
For the gay beams of lightsome day
Gild, but to flout, the ruins grey.
When the broken arches are black in night,
And each shafted oriel glimmers white;
Where the cold light's uncertain shower
Streams on the ruin'd central tower;
When buttress and buttress, alternately,
Seem framed of ebon and ivory;
When silver edges the imagery,
And the scrolls that teach thee to live and die;
When distant Tweed is heard to rave,
And the owlet to hoot o'er the dead man's grave,
Then go − but go alone the while −
Then view St David's ruin'd pile;
And, home returning, soothly swear,
Was never scene so sad and fair!

Sir Walter Scott, *The Lay of the Last Minstrel* (1805)

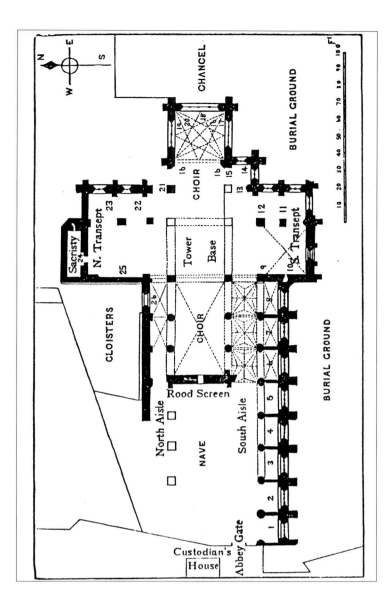

MELROSE ABBEY

THE GROUND PLAN ILLUSTRATED.

VISITORS on entering St Mary's are respectfully requested to keep to the right hand all round.

Nos. 1 to 8—Chapels facing south aisle.

9 and 10—Door of stair, and John Murdo's inscription.

11 and 12—St Bridget's Chapel and statue, still standing.

13—Chapel.

14—Tomb of Michael Scott, the "Wizard," according to the "Lay."

15—Tomb of Sir Ralph Ivers or Evers, killed at Ancrum Moor, 1545, and probably "Latoun lies here also.

16—Chancel.

17—Tomb of Alexander II. (petrified tombstone).

18—Rest of the heart of Robert the Bruce.

19 and 20—William Douglas, "the dark Knight of Liddesdale"; Douglas the hero of Otterburn, or "Chevy Chase"; and many of this heroic and illustrious race, were interred here.

21—Chapel, north-east end destroyed.

22 and 23—St Stephen's Chapel.

24—Entrance to Sacristy. Under the lower step is the tomb of Queen Johanna, wife of Alexander II.

25—Font at foot of Abbot's staircase.

26—Cloister door. To the left of it, on the wall, the inscription, "Here lies the race of the House of Zair" (Yair). Opposite are the tombs of the ancient family of Karr, Kar, Ker, Kerr, of Kippilaw.

This year's daylight service to Portrush by the handsome screw steamer *Azalea* of the Laird Line started on Tuesday, with Captain Beattie in command. Quite a large number of passengers took advantage of the opening cruise. Leaving Ardrossan at 10 a.m., the *Azalea* arrives in Portrush about four o'clock in the afternoon. The sail is a very pleasant and interesting one. Land is never lost sight of, and a capital view is caught in passing of the basaltic pyramids of the famed Giants' Causeway. Portrush, which used to be a small fishing village, has now all the comforts and conveniences of a city, with numerous fine hotels, boarding-houses, and ample boating and bathing facilities. The business of the place, however, seems to be golfing. I understand, indeed, that the links are the most famous of any in Ireland.

On the arrival of the steamer at the quay the jaunting car is strongly in evidence, and trips can be made in the afternoon to many pleasant places in the vicinity. Altogether, there is no pleasanter two-days' trip – economical and comfortable – than the daylight trip to Portrush.

On the opening run the comfort of the passengers was courteously looked after by Mr Struthers, the superintending steward of the company.

Clyde Shipping Report, 1903

The custodian John Hood and his wife wait at the gateway of the ruined twelfth-century Cistercian Abbey of St Mary at Melrose, Roxburghshire. To the right stands the now vanished Abbey Hotel, and to the left the long-demolished thatched cottage and souvenir shop of the custodian.

The Loch Tay, Perthshire, steamer Maid of the Loch, *edging past Kenmore Pier. Kenmore manse is in the background. The loch is 14½ miles long with fine views of Ben Lawers; the steamer route was from Killin to Kenmore, via Ardeonaig, Lawers, Ardtalnaig and Fearnan.*

Boys congregate to ogle the cameraman at the Mercat Cross, Cupar, Fife, 1903. The lamps were removed during the First World War. Cupar is the old county town of Fife. The Mercat Cross was re-erected on this site in 1897 to commemorate Queen Victoria's Diamond Jubilee.

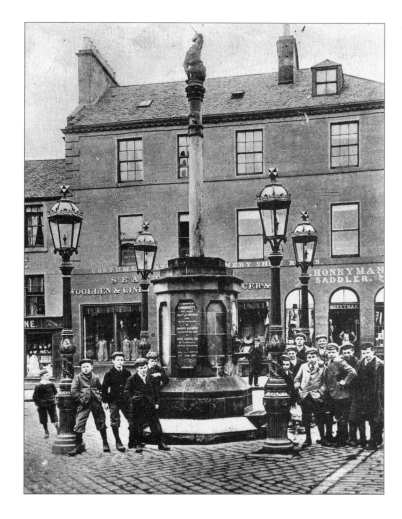

Postcard view of Wellmeadow, Blairgowrie, Perthshire, at the junction of Gas Brae and Allan Street, soon after the erection of the fountain in 1893.

A GERMAN NOVELIST'S VISIT TO
KILLIECRANKIE, 1858

The Pass of Killiecrankie is of importance for three reasons – it is a means of communication, it is a place of exceptional scenic beauty and finally it is of importance because of the bloody battle that was fought here on 27th July 1689 between the followers of the Stuarts under Claverhouse and the troops of William of Orange.

The general picture presented by the pass reminds one vividly of the Trossachs. These have a greater reputation for beauty and are visited annually by thousands for their own sake, while only those get to know the Pass of Killiecrankie who are led by inclination or business to the actual north of Scotland. You go through it because you have to. It is a way but not a goal. This indisputable fact is an injustice.

The Pass of Killiecrankie is more imposing than the Trossachs. The reason for this seems to me to be that the walls of rock are closer to one another and confront each other more steeply, that the Garry is every inch a loud and rushing mountain torrent and enlivens the romantic scene much more than the insignificant little stream which seems to crawl rather than to foam through the Trossachs; finally, the preponderance of deciduous trees over pines decides the contest in favour of the Killiecrankie Pass. Moreover the bloody battle that took place here, and was a thing of far greater importance than half a dozen clan wars with the sheep- and cattle-stealing MacGregors, should surely have been of advantage to the more northerly spot. But the descriptions of Walter Scott, who saw fit to set the scene of his story on the shore of Lake Katrine, decided the matter in favour of the Trossachs once for all, and so long as *The Lady of the Lake* continues to have enthusiastic admirers in every corner of the world, for so long will the Pass of Killiecrankie have to be reconciled to the relinquishment of its right of primogeniture in favour of its younger brother.

I stood upright in the vehicle (needless to say on one foot) when we drove up the pass. The whole picture was so charming that I was anxious to lose nothing of its beauty. Now and then the Garry, foaming below us, withdrew from our gaze and only our ear perceived its presence; then once again we saw it foaming over the rocky terrain in broad waterfalls that were like great stone stairways.

When we had almost reached the northern end of the pass the conductor put his hand on my shoulder and called out while making a motion to the right with his head: 'Look, there is the battlefield!' And there it was, half in front of us and half beside us, no bigger than a village green or the

W.H. Bartlett's 1859 interpretation of the Pass of Killiecrankie, the defile through which the River Garry forces its way to join the River Tummel. This view encouraged Victorian and Edwardian artists, both amateur and professional, to set up their easels.

'The Field of Killiecrankie', where John Graham of Claverhouse, Viscount Dundee (1648–89), mortally wounded, defeated the royalist Williamite forces of General Hugh MacKay on 27 July 1689. The upright stone marks where 'Bonnie Dundee' fell.

playground of an English school. The shape of the place is oblong. We drove along one of the longer sides, the other three being densely lined with deciduous trees.

At what was more or less the most northerly point of the field we became aware of a stone standing upright and about the size of an ordinary gate-post. This is the place where fell the victor of that day – William [John] Graham, Duke of Claverhouse and Marquis of Dundee. Concerning that victory and the person of the victor, I may be permitted here to say the following.

Among the partisans who, after the removal of James II (1688), made the cause of the Stuarts their own, Graham of Claverhouse, Viscount Dundee, or 'Bonnie Dundee', as he is called in the Jacobite song, overtops all the rest. What the great Montrose had been forty years previously in the days of Charles I – the champion of loyalty and royalty against Whiggish Puritanism – such was now 'Bonnie Dundee' after the Stuarts had been driven out. Even while James II was still on the throne he had uncompromisingly taken the part of the little-loved King and now, after the latter's fall, he was the first to gather the Highland clans around him and to declare war on the government in London.

Like Montrose, he belonged to the clan of the Grahams, a name which during the second half of the seventeenth century should be associated with the idea of an irrevocable royalist outlook, even as the name of Argyle should suggest inveterate Puritanism. For fifty years fortune favoured now one and now the other of the two parties, both of which were filled with deadly hatred for each other, and the heads of both all too often found opportunity to seal their faith and their devotion by death. At the same place where the heads

of the Argyles fell as a result of their faithfulness to Puritanism, there too fell the head of the great Montrose in the service of his King.

'Bonnie Dundee', however, more fortunate than the majority of the party heads at that time, died a hero's death on the field of Killiecrankie in the very moment when victory had crowned his cause. As he was rushing forward with arm upraised in pursuit of the flying foe, a bullet hit him in the armpit and killed him on the spot. The upright stone of which I spoke marks the spot where he fell. With his fall came, for the time being at least, the end of the Stuart chances. The victory which he had won ceased to be a victory. The Whigs triumphed; their bitterest enemy, whom they had till then looked upon as invincible and immune against wounds, was no more. The belief in this immunity, which needless to say, was supposed to have been due to a pact with the devil, was at that time widespread among Scottish folk. It was said that cold water began to steam and to hiss whenever Dundee put his feet into it, and that the ball which ultimately struck him was not a bullet at all but a silver button which one of his servants had removed from his master's coat and shot at him. *Only what came from himself could reach him.*

Dundee's sword is at present in the possession of Lord Woodhouselee and has been preserved at Penicuik House near Edinburgh. The memory of his victories is still alive in Scotland and a certain catchword is still used in regard to any situation which appears to call for a helper: 'Only half an hour of Dundee.'

Theodore Fontane, *Jenseits des Tweed: Bilder und Briefe aus Schottland* (1860)

LOCKED UP AMONG THE MEMORIALS
GREYFRIARS CHURCHYARD, EDINBURGH

As if there had been some destiny in the matter, the Greyfriars Churchyard became connected with another remarkable event in the religious troubles of the seventeenth century. At the south-west angle, accessible by an old gateway bearing emblems of mortality, and which is fitted with an iron-rail gate of very old workmanship, is a kind of supplement to the burying-ground – an oblong space, now having a line of sepulchral enclosures on each side, but formerly empty. On these enclosures the visitor may remark, as he passes, certain names venerable in the history of science and of letters; as, for instance, Joseph Black and Alexander Tytler. On one he sees the name of Gilbert Innes of Stow, who left a million, to take six feet of earth here. These, however, do not form the matter in point. Every lesser particular becomes trivial beside the extraordinary use to which the place was put by the Government in the year 1679. Several hundred of the prisoners taken at Bothwell Bridge were confined here in the open air, under circumstances of privation now scarcely credible. They had hardly anything either to lie upon or to cover them; their allowance of provision was four ounces of bread per day,

with water derived from one of the city pipes, which passed near the place. They were guarded by day by eight and through the night by twenty-four men; and the soldiers were told that if any prisoner escaped, they should answer it life for life by cast of dice. If any prisoner rose from the ground by night, he was shot at. Women alone were permitted to commune with them, and bring them food or clothes; but these had often to stand at the entrance from morning till night without getting access, and were frequently insulted and maltreated by the soldiers, without the prisoners being able to protect them, although in many cases related by the most endearing ties. In the course of several weeks a considerable number of the prisoners had been liberated upon signing a bond, in which they promised never again to take up arms against the king or without his authority; but it appears that about four hundred, refusing mercy on such terms, were kept in this frightful bivouac for five months, being only allowed at the approach of winter to have shingle huts erected over them, which was boasted of as a great mercy. Finally, on the 15th of November, a remnant, numbering two hundred and fifty-seven, were put on board a ship to be sent to Barbados. The vessel was wrecked on one of the Orkney Islands, when only about forty came ashore alive.

Scotland's Victorians took an increasing interest in sculpture, much of it of a memorial nature for the huge town cemeteries, known as Cities of the Dead. Here, at his Garnethill studio a Glasgow sculptor pauses to admire his work in 1880.

From the gloom of this sad history there is shed one ray of romance. Amongst the charitable women of Edinburgh who came to minister to the prisoners, there was one attended by a daughter – a young and, at least by right of romance, a fair girl. Every few days they approached this iron gate with food and clothes, either from their own stores or collected among neighbours. Between the young lady and one of the juvenile prisoners an attachment sprang up. Doubtless she loved him for the dangers he had passed in so good a cause, and he loved her because she pitied them. In happier days, long after, when their constancy had been well tried by an exile which he suffered in the plantations, this pair were married, and settled in Edinburgh, where they had sons and daughters.

Robert Chambers, *Traditions of Edinburgh* (1824)

THE MURDER OF ARCHBISHOP JAMES SHARP

The royalist Archbishop Sharp was looked upon as a traitor by those who adhered to the Scottish National Covenant (on religious liberty) of 1638. An attempt had already been made on his life in 1668; a Victorian chronicler takes up the story of the famous assassination . . .

This unhappy man, one of the prime movers of the recent oppression and misgovernment of the country, and the merciless persecutor of his former associates, had long been the object of deep hatred on the part of the great body of the people. He was regarded not merely as a selfish, haughty, tyrannical prelate – a Judas – a treacherous and perjured apostate, but as a person of superhuman wickedness, an agent of the devil, who frequently appeared to him in a bodily shape. A worthless fellow named Carmichael had been employed by the primate as one of his chief agents to prosecute the nonconformists in Fife, and by the cruel tortures which he had inflicted upon the wives, children, and servants of the intercommuned, that they might be compelled to reveal where their relations were concealed, had rendered himself so obnoxious to the covenanters that nine of their number, chiefly belonging to the class of small proprietors, resolved to inflict exemplary punishment upon him for his barbarities. Accordingly, on the 3rd of May, 1679, this exasperated band, headed by David Hackston, of Rathillet, and his brother-in-law, John Balfour of Burley, waylaid Carmichael near the town of Cupar; but, having been forewarned of his danger, he contrived to escape. Disappointed in their search for the

Murder stories were given full rein in Scotland's newspapers and broadsheets in the nineteenth century. Tour guides, too, were quick to point out the locations and gory details of Scotland's most celebrated murders. On 3 May 1679 James Sharp, the 61-year-old Archbishop of St Andrews, was murdered by Covenanters at Magus Muir, Strathkinness, Fife.

instrument of so much suffering, they were about to separate, when a farmer's wife sent a boy to tell them that the archbishop himself was approaching, on his return from Edinburgh to St Andrews. In their excited and fanatical state of mind they instantly interpreted this incident as a divine call to 'execute that justice which the law denied them,' against the persecutor of God's people. 'It was immediately suggested,' says one of them, 'that albeit we had missed the man we sought for, yet God had by a wonderful providence delivered the great and capital enemy of his Church into our hands, and that it was a visible call to us from heaven not to let him escape.' They accordingly pursued and overtook the primate upon Magus Moor, about three miles from St Andrews, and, having cut the traces, and disarmed and dismounted his attendants, they ordered him to come out of the coach. On his refusal they fired into the carriage, his daughter, who was seated by his side all the while, piteously imploring mercy. One of the assassins named Russell opened the coach-door, and ordered Sharp to come out. 'I take God to witness,' he added, 'that it is not out of any hatred to your person, nor for any prejudice you have done or could have done me, that I intend now to take your life, but because you have been, and still continue to be, an avowed opposer of the Gospel and kingdom of Christ, and a murderer of his saints, whose blood you have shed like water.' At length, after being wounded by a sword thrust, the old man left the coach, and, creeping on his knees towards one of the band whom he recognised, said 'You are a gentleman – you will protect me!' But the person addressed turned away, saying, 'I will not lay a hand upon you.' One of the assassins, probably Hackston, relenting, cried to the rest, 'Spare those grey hairs.' Sharp himself poured out entreaties for life, promised them an indemnity, offered them money, and even engaged to lay down his office if they would but spare him. But he was in the hands of men who were steeled against his supplications by a passion stronger even than revenge. They reminded him of his promise to Mitchell, upbraided him as an enemy to God and his people, and then pierced him with innumerable wounds. His daughter, who threw herself between her father and his murderers, and made the most frantic efforts to save his life, also received several wounds in the struggle. After rifling the coach of the arms and papers which it contained, the assassins rode off unmolested, leaving the lifeless and mangled body of their victim on the moor.

James Taylor, *The Pictorial History of Scotland* (1859)

In Holy Trinity Kirk looms the vast towering monument of Archbishop James Sharpe, extending right up to the roof, one of the finest and most interesting tombs in Scotland. The work was executed in black and white marble by a Dutch sculptor, at the expense of the dead primate's son, and for some time existed only precariously; for the Covenanters,

A highlight for nineteenth-century visitors to Holy Trinity Church, St Andrews, was the tomb and monument to the murdered Archbishop Sharp in the Sharp Aisle. Many such memorials were refurbished in Victorian times. Queen Victoria herself paid for the renovation of several royal tombs in Scotland.

being determined to deal with the tomb as they had dealt with the dead man under it, more than once mustered at Magus Muir, proposing to march on St Andrews and demolish the monument. The Sharpes, however, had attached to the tomb an annual mortification for the maintenance of the monument and the relief of the parish poor; and the canny St Andreans, therefore, always turned out in force to repel the iconoclasts. In 1725, nevertheless, some men broke into the church and did damage to the archbishop's sepulchre; but it has been repaired, and is handsome today. (The luckless primate's bones, however, seem to have been carried off by the desecrators.) There are Fife folk still who have queasy consciences about its being allowed to dominate a Presbyterian kirk: I once heard an old man guiding friends through Holy Trinity remark, nodding toward the great tomb, 'That's from popish times. There's some say it no should be here.'

In the high pediment, the primate of Scotland props a church; below, two angels with extended wings uphold shield, mitre, and crosiers. Between splendid Corinthian columns the graven image of Dr Sharpe, carved in the round, kneels upon his sarcophagus; from a cloud executed in white marble, an angel extends a martyr's crown above the archbishop's head, so that he may exchange his mitre for a crown: *pro mitra coronam* became the motto of the Sharpes thereafter. Upon the pedestal at the monument's base is depicted, in low relief, the dreadful scene of the murder of Sharpe: the 'nine sworn fanatic parricides' hacking mercilessly at the fallen primate, whose distraught daughter struggles in the background, near a coach. ('What mutterest thou of grey hairs?' cries the raving Burley, in his cave, this scene recurring to his mind in *Old Mortality*. 'It was well done to slay him – the more ripe the corn the readier for the sickle.') Upon the black sarcophagus, the epitaph declares that 'This lofty tomb covers the unspeakably precious dust of the holiest of bishops, the sagest of state-counsellors, the most saintly of martyrs.'

Russell Kirk, *St Andrews* (1954)

ARCHBISHOP SHARP'S EPITAPH

To the Lord God, supreme ruler of the world. This lofty tomb covers the unspeakably precious dust of the holiest of bishops, the sagest of state-councillors, the most saintly of martyrs, for here lies all that remains beneath the sun of the Most Reverend Father in Christ, James Sharp, Doctor of Divinity, Archbishop of St Andrews, Primate of all Scotland, etc., whom the University regarded, acknowledged and continually marvelled at as a professor of theology and philosophy, the Church as priest, teacher and leader, Scotland as its Prime Minister ecclesiastical and lay, Britain as the advocate of the restoration of His Most Gracious Majesty, Charles the Second, and of the monarchy, the world of Christianity as the man who re-established the order of Episcopacy in Scotland, good and faithful subjects as a model of piety, and angel of peace, an oracle of wisdom and a picture of dignity, enemies of God, the King and the people as the bitterest foe of irreligion, treason and schism, and whom despite his character and eminence nine sworn assassins, inspired by fanatical rage, did with pistols, swords and daggers foully massacre close to his metropolitan seat, under the noonday sun . . .

VERSES FROM A VICTORIAN LADY'S EPITAPH BOOK

J.J., died 1734.

At this cold pillow lies her head,
And hopes to raise with Jacob's seed;
Prudent she was in virtue's walk,
And to do good in moderate talk.

Biggar Churchyard

Monument to George Augustus Frederick John Murray, 6th Duke of Atholl (1814–64), at Dunkeld, Perthshire. This is the unveiling ceremony, by his wife Duchess Anne, in 1866.

April, 1664

Heir lyes Four vertous Vimen. Al Spouses to Johne Dov, of Lammerkin. The first caled Marjorie Dov, Catharin Burdin, Annas Ridheuch, and Janet Lindsay.

Aberdalgie Churchyard, Perthshire

Here lies the dust of Grisal Jarden, 1782.
Hark from the tombs a doleful sound,
My God, attend the cry,
Ye living men, come view the ground,
Where you must shortly lye.
Princes, this clay must shortly be your bed,
In spite of all your tours,
All the wise reverend heads,
Must lie as low as ours.

Wiston Churchyard, Lanarkshire

High Street, Strathmiglo, Fife, looking towards the Townhouse and Steeple (1734), c. 1910. By the early 1800s hand-weaving prospered in the village, only to be replaced by power looms as the century evolved.

In memory of M.S., died 1773, aged 4 years; also M.S., died 1775, aged 3 years; also D.S., died 1778, aged 2 years.

Beneath this stone, in silent sleep,
Two loving Infants rest,
Whose Parents' rising joys, By death,
Alas, were soon supprest;
By water's force their thread of life
Was early cut in twain,
Tho' still we weep, still we rejoice
To think we'll meet again.
Tho' they are gone we live in hope
That they again shall rise,
When the last Trumpet's solemn sound
Shall call them to the skys,
From a base world where tumults rage
And tiresome jars ne'er cease,
Where frends are foes, increasing woes,
'Tis hop'd they rest in peace.

Kirkmahoe Churchyard

When all thy mercies, O my God,
My rising soul surveys,
Transported with the view I'm lost
In wonder, love, and praise.

Skirling Churchyard

In memory of J.G., Student of Physic, who perished in the River Nith on the 22nd day of July, 1782, aged 23 years. Having attained a proficiency in Literature and Science, and an extensive knowledge in the art of Physic, he fell, lamented by his friends, and sincerely regretted by all who knew him.

Endu'd with genius and with learning stor'd,
The arduous haunts of Science he explor'd;
Fair Friendship, Truth sincere, and sense refin'd,
Blended their influence in his lib'ral mind;
Each social virtue did her powers impart,
To raise, enlarge, and harmonize his heart.
Still must his friends his fate with sorrow bear,
And sad Remembrance force the pitying tear.

Mouswald Churchyard

Thomas C., died Sept. 18th, 1763, aged 24; William C., died Sept. 18th, 1763.

Think not, young men,
On threescore ten,
Or yet on long fourscore,
But quit the stage,
At any age,
As these have done before.

Trailflat Churchyard

J.M., died August 31st, 1708, aged 50.

If grace, good manners, gifts of mind,
Yea where all moral virtues have combined,
Compleat a man, behold beneath this stone,
Here lyes intered, whom rich and poor bemoan,
He run his race, abundant entrance got,
His name is Savori, and shall not rot.

St Michael's Churchyard, Dumfries

J.M.

Death wounds to cure, we fall, we rise, we reign,
Spring from our fetters, fasten in the skies
Where blooming Eden withers in our sight,
The King of Terrors is the Prince of Peace.

St Michael's Churchyard, Dumfries

Erected to the Memory of Gordon Fraser, who wrote songs and poems on Wigtown.

O bury me at Wigtown,
And o'er me raise a modest stane,
Tae tell the folks when I am gane,
The cauld mools wrap the banes o' ane
Wha' wrote and sang o' Wigtown.

Wigtown

Lady Johnson-Ferguson, *Epitaphs* (1913)

BRIGHT REFLECTIONS ON THE VILLAGE OF DULL

Physical Basis. The *New Statistical Account* gives a full description of the Parish of Dull as it was in 1842. Much recorded there regarding geography is of permanent reference, but very considerable change has taken place since then, both in the bounds of the parish and in the manner of the life of its people. In 1891 the civil parish, till that time composed of three separate areas was unified by the Boundary Commissioners, who transferred the intervening territory to Dull. Thus, along the Tay, Dull received from Logierait parish, part of Aberfeldy and land south-west of that town; from Fortingall, the Bolfracks district; from Weem, Comrie Castle and adjacent ground on both sides of the Tay. In Glen Quaich, detached parts of Weem and Kenmore parishes were also annexed to Dull. At the same time Dull gave up to Blair Atholl all it held north of Loch Tummel and the River Tummel, i.e. Fincastle, etc.; to Logierait it yielded the Grandtully district; and to Weem, the Derculich and Glassie district. So altered, the parish is some 16 miles long from north to south and 4 to 9 miles wide, the land area being 55,926 acres. It has Blair Atholl parish to the north; Moulin, Logierait, Weem, and Little Dunkeld parishes to the east; Fowlis Wester and the parish of Monzievaird and Strowan to the south; Kenmore and Fortingall to the west. The River Tummel and Loch Tummel bound the parish in the north; the Tay flows across the middle; the mountain ridge between Glen Quaich and Glen Almond forms the southern boundary.

The eternal hills look down upon our straths as of yore, and the Tay, the Lyon, the Braan, and the Tummel wind their seaward way, deepening their channels, yet not sufficiently to counteract flooding, which sometimes interferes with agriculture and communication. Wade's Bridge at Aberfeldy fulfils its useful function, and the Comrie Bridge, for which the writer of the *New Statistical Account* sighed, has been built. Motors have almost entirely superseded the old horse traffic, but as a compensation the roads have been vastly improved.

History. Relics of ancient duns and camps still exist; druidical circles and stones survive in a mutilated state; and the Cross of Dull witnesses to an earlier time when the fugitive had to be protected from hot-headed justice by sanctuary. The 'big houses' continue to dot the landscape, but under very different conditions, some fast falling into decay, with their glories becoming a memory. Great changes have taken place in the composition of the community. The outstanding fact and regret is the depopulation of the district, which still goes on. Where there were once considerable hamlets there are now only residuary groups, or indeed no human life at all. Few signs are left of the feudal times. Land-holding has dwindled, and is now confined to the immediate acreage of the 'big houses' and the grouse moors attached. The farms tend to be largely in the hands and ownership of the farmers, who have been constrained to buy outright. This is an interesting situation, instancing the 'circle come round' in human affairs.

The landward part of the parish is controlled by the county council, in supersession of the local courts of the Justices of the Peace which formerly held sway, though the licensing courts and some other interests are still in their hands. Aberfeldy, on the other hand is a police burgh, having been constituted so in 1887, but criminal matters are referred to the Sheriff Court at Perth. The county council has in hand the roads, education, and some other liabilities in Aberfeldy, but otherwise the burgh is administered by the town council of nine men and women, who elect their provost. It is interesting to record that Provost J.D. Haggart has recently retired after 46 years' continuous service as councillor, during 36 of which he had served as provost. This may well be regarded a record in municipal history.

Revd James D. Mitchell, *Parish of Dull* (1950)

The village of Dull, Perthshire, from the south-west, c. 1890. Many such villages had thrived in medieval times, but fell to poverty by the nineteenth century. There was a long tradition that there had been a Celtic monastery here which offered 'university education', and that Celtic clergy from Dull transferred their school to St Andrews.

A golf competition between James Braid (1870–1950) – five times Open Champion 1901–10 – and Henry 'Harry' Vardon (1870–1937) – six times Open Champion – on 25 September 1901, at Vertish Hill, Hawick golf course.

THE FINISH OF THE DRIVE.

HENRY VARDON

The Famous Golfer

ADDITIONAL interest is given to the open champion golf match at Prestwick, on Wednesday and Thursday, by the appearance of Harry Vardon on the links. Vardon is one of the heroes of the world of golf. Indeed, he is regarded by many as the leading golfer in all the world. Born at Glouville, in the Island of Jersey, he has newly entered his thirty-fourth year. He early took to golf. By and by he became known outwith the Channel Islands as a player. His first engagement was with the Ripon Club as greenkeeper. Then he went to Bury in a similar capacity, and in Bury he remained for three years. In 1896, '98, and '99 he won the open championship of Great Britain. His play has not gone off since the last-named year, but it is remarked that Taylor, Braid, and Herd, the champions of 1900, 1901, and 1902 – Vardon being second each year – have improved to something like his level. Writing on Vardon, Horace Hutchison, whose pursuits are golf and literature, but especially golf, says: 'Vardon's temperature as a golfer seems to have all the qualities of his style – qualities that seem to have very few defects attaching to them. The quietness and control of his swing are reflected in the modest confidence of his manner. He is universally, we believe, liked as a man; universally, we are sure, feared as a golfer.'

The Bailie Cartoon Supplement, 10 June 1903

FARMING MATTERS

The Industrial Revolution was accompanied by a great advance in agriculture. The way was prepared by two Acts of 1695 for the division of common lands, and the separation of intermixed properties. Early in the eighteenth century (1723) was formed a 'Society of Improvers in the Knowledge of Agriculture in Scotland,' one member of which, John, 2nd Earl of Stair, is said to have been the first to cultivate turnips in Scotland. White oats and wheat began to replace coarse black oats and bere; potatoes were introduced, and Dr Johnson found them even in Skye; agricultural machinery, and the breeds of cattle, sheep, and horses were greatly improved.

The progress in communications, too, by which this century was also signalised, encouraged the conveyance of agricultural produce to markets, and the extended use of lime as a manure. The abolition of hereditary jurisdictions (1746) after the Jacobite rebellion, and an Act of 1770 giving the landlords power to grant leases, with the spread of enclosures, drainage, and rotation of crops, made the country ready to benefit by the great rise in the price of wheat during the French Revolutionary Wars, though in the Highlands there was much depopulation when the chiefs, their bond with their clansmen broken, forced emigration in the interests of sheep farms. As a result there was an enormous advance in Scottish agriculture, and the rental of land rose from £2,000,000 in 1795 to £5,278,685 in 1815. The last quarter of the nineteenth century, however, saw the beginning of the importation of great quantities of foreign and colonial wheat, and this proved to be competition which British agriculture could not meet. A comparison of the census returns for the first years of the nineteenth and twentieth centuries shows that the increase in the population of Scotland during that period from rather over one and a half millions to nearly four and a half has taken place in the counties most affected by the Industrial Revolution. The increase per square mile in Lanark is 1357, in Midlothian 1001, in Renfrew 811, Linlithgow 416, Clackmannan 370, Dumbarton 346, Fife 252, Forfar 215, Stirling 206, and Ayr 151. Ten more counties have an increase of between 100 and 20 per square mile; and eight, Dumfries, Caithness, Kirkcudbright, Nairn, Orkney and Shetland, Inverness, Ross and Cromarty, and Berwick, an increase of less than 20. An actual decrease of population has taken place in Sutherland, Kinross, Argyll, and Perth. Undoubtedly this feature of modern life, the concentration of population into great towns, is from many points of view a dangerous one. The Scotsman's wandering impulse, too, which from the fifteenth to eighteenth century filled the armies and universities of Europe, and is, for instance, so marked both in the life and in the books of a writer so essentially Scots as Robert Louis Stevenson, has found revival

Haymaking at Strathallan Castle, Perthshire, c. 1860. Three of the daughters of the laird, the Hon. William Henry Drummond, are to the right. At this date haymaking tools were still primitive and work was labour-intensive.

The main street, Elie, Fife, looking east, from a popular postcard of the day. Note the lack of traffic, street furniture, telephone and telegraph wires.

NATIONAL TELEPHONE SERVICE.

THE LARGEST WORKING SYSTEM.

THE MOST EFFICIENT SERVICE.

RATES TO SUIT ALL CLASSES OF TELEPHONE USERS.

SPECIAL TRUNK CONNECTION RATE FOR LARGE USERS, £5 PER ANNUM.

PARTY LINE SERVICE, FROM 25s PER ANNUM.

FOR FULL PARTICULARS, APPLY TO THE CONTRACT DEPARTMENT, ROYAL EXCHANGE.

TELEPHONES ${5000 \atop 5001}$ ROYAL.

in the first quarter of the twentieth century in the heavy drain of much of the best of Scotland's population to the colonies. This is another serious problem for those who care that Scotland should have a future as well as the Empire as a whole. One thing, however, is certain. It is quite contrary to the fixed intention characteristic of this type of Scotsman to 'get on,' to expect that he will be content to stay at home, either on the land or in the cities, if he has no chance to realise his ambition.

W.R. Kermack, *Historical Geography of Scotland* (1926)

THE ELECTRIC TELEGRAPH

The introduction of the electric telegraph naturally aroused much curiosity in the rural population as to how the wires could carry messages. A West Highlander who had been to Glasgow and was consequently supposed to have got to the bottom of the mystery, was asked to explain it. 'Weel,' said he, 'it's no easy to explain what you will no be understandin'. But I'll tell ye what it's like. If you could stretch my collie dog frae Oban to Tobermory, an' if you wass to clap its head in Oban, an' it waggit its tail in Tobermory, or if I wass to tread on its tail in Oban an' it squaked in Tobermory – that's what the telegraph is like.'

Sir Archibald Geikie

The market by St John's Church, Perth, at the turn of the century. The capital of Scotland until around 1452, Perth was a thriving city of dye-works, distilleries and breweries a hundred years ago.

TURNIPS VERSUS STEAKS

Turnip steaks, bean pie, and tea don't appear to be just the sort of dieting that a man who intends to walk a thousand miles in 20 days should go in for. Mr G.H. Allen, the vegetarian-teetotal pedestrian, who started from the Glasgow Royal Exchange, on the 25th of last month on a tramp to London by a serpentine route, covering ten hundred miles, got the length of Doncaster – about half the distance – last Thursday, when he had to give in. A beef-eating gentleman, who is not averse to something more potent than tea, is understood to be in training for the feat, and 6 to 4 is being asked (latest quotations) on his chance of accomplishing it.

News Item, 1903

BEWARE THE VILLAGE GHOSTS

I well remember, when as a lad of eighteen I first visited Skye, that the steamer carrying the usual miscellaneous cargo in the hold and on deck, after rounding the Mull had made so many

A circus on the move in the Border Country between Melrose and Galashiels. Camels and elephants pause on Melrose Road, Galashiels, c. 1900.

Sets of postcards became popular as the craze for collecting them grew in Scotland from the 1870s. Local postcard producers like George L. Fleming of St Andrews made many sets like these. The card shows Lumbo Farm, outside St Andrews.

Hell Bunker, Hole No. 14 'The Long', Old Course, St Andrews. The earliest surviving document about golf in St Andrews dates from 1553 and three hundred years later it had become the Mecca of golfers.

Melbourne Place, St Andrews.

calls, and had so much luggage and merchandise to discharge at each halt, that it was past midnight of the second day before we came into Broadford Bay. The disembarkation was by small-boat, and as we made our way shorewards, the faces of the oarsmen were at every stroke lit up with the pale, ghostly light of a phosphorescent sea. The night was dark, but with the aid of a dim lantern one could mount the rough beach, where I was met by a son of the Revd John Mackinnon of Kilbride, with whom I had come to spend a few weeks. We had a drive of some five miles inland, enlivened with Gaelic songs which my young friend and his cousin screamed at the pitch of their voices. At a certain part of the road they became suddenly silent, or only spoke to each other in whispers. We were then passing the old graveyard at Kilchrist; but when we had got to what was judged a safe distance beyond it and its ghosts, the hilarity began anew, and lasted until we came to our destination between two and three o'clock in the morning.

Sir Archibald Geikie

Chapter 4

THE PEOPLE'S PYRAMID

T*he layers of society in Victorian and Edwardian Scotland were formed as a pyramid. At the top was the monarch, with the aristocracy as the royal footstool. Next came the wealthy upper middle class, with their mines, factories, distilleries and shipyards, followed closely by the merchants and traders, the lower middle-class clerks and corner shopkeepers, all looked down upon as being 'in trade' by the middle-class denizens who followed a profession. And at the base stood the common folk who had their own social hierarchy of skilled upper working class, the unskilled, the 'deserving poor', the destitute (those who had no means of raising credit) and the 'dregs of humanity'.*

Within this pyramid too, were layers of the privileged, who had achieved their positions, honour, and social status either by personal influence, or through being democratically elected to civic positions as provosts (the equivalent of the English mayor), bailies (the Scots magistrates who presided in borough courts and were elected by a town council from among the councillors) and councillors. All, however, were in tune with the spirit of the age.

Scots folk of one hundred years ago were not like modern folk:

they spoke differently, their streets and persons smelled different, and they thought differently. They had a strong confidence in the way they lived, worshipped, carried out their business, and regarded the world, and they were travelling in unison along the road towards success, prosperity and peace. In their society the main aim was to be respectable. This meant that Scots society in general was easily shocked whether by speech or behaviour. Thus the whole nation was scandalised when an eccentric Scots peer, the 8th Marquess of Queensberry, precipitated the Oscar Wilde prosecution for indecency in 1895. There was a striving, too, for conformity, particularly among the lower orders.

In 1897 Scots folk could look back on how they had developed into a world-beating nation alongside the teenage girl who had become their Queen in 1837. The monarch symbolised the glorious achievements of the British nation, among whom the Scots – with few exceptions – then numbered themselves; the Queen's jubilee of that year was a joyful acknowledgement of national self-esteem and pride in an empire upon which the sun never set.

One hundred years ago Scotland's society remained rigidly structured, with the sexes prescribed their individual roles. Here, in a flourish of distinctive fashions of the day, members of the Coldingham Church Women's Guild pose on Coldingham Sands, 1908.

Scotland was then a nation without state-provided welfare, ruled by a parliament (in England) consisting largely of aristocratic grandees, but the Scots nevertheless demonstrated a passionate patriotism, particularly on the field of battle – from the Crimean (1854–6) and Zulu (1879) wars, to those of the Sudan (1896) and the First World War (1914–18) – in a manner hard to comprehend one hundred years later. They felt superiority over foreigners, but when King Edward VII played a key role in forging the Entente Cordiale (1904), after years of Anglo-French rivalry, he was following in the footsteps of the age-old Scots' 'Auld Alliance' with France. Yet there were undercurrents of radicalism and rebellion as the underprivileged began to realise the power of their combined social cooperation which was soon to be expressed in civil disobedience.

George Burnett (1822–90), Scottish lawyer, historian and heraldic author, and Lord Lyon King-of-Arms from 1866 to 1890. The Lord Lyon is the highest ranking of all heralds and has armorial jurisdiction throughout the Kingdom of Scotland. He is a king with his own crown and, as one historian put it, 'he is the custodian of that Spirit of Caledonia which is allegorically incarnate in the Queen'. Scotland was an early player in the realm of armorial heraldry within Western Europe. Once Scotland had thirteen royal officers-of-arms, but in 1867 this number was reduced to seven: the Lord Lyon, three Heralds and three Pursuivants, all of whom are members of the Scottish Royal Household. Scots coats of arms are logged in the Lyon Register and legal disputes concerning the ownership of such family arms is initially settled in the Lyon Court.

SCOTLAND'S OWN ORDER OF CHIVALRY

One hundred years ago and more there was a great outpouring of interest in 'things Scottish', with a resurgence of popularity in Scottish antiques and Scottish symbolism, from Saltires to Thistles. Queen Victoria was much taken with the Scottish Thistle plant and the 4th Earl of Clarendon, the Foreign Secretary, remarked on the thistle motif on the wallpaper at Balmoral that there were enough 'in the drawing-room alone to choke a donkey'.

The Most Ancient and Most Noble Order of the Thistle, now limited to the sovereign and sixteen knights by the statute of 1827, was revived and promulgated by statute of King James VII & II on 29 May 1687. Tradition averred that it was founded by Achaius, King of the Scots, to honour the Patron Saint of Scotland, the Apostle and Martyr St Andrew of Bethsaida in Galilee, in 809. The Order fell out of use at the end of James's reign but was revived by Queen Anne on 31 December 1703. Its intent was to give Scotland an Order comparable to that of the Garter of England. It is awarded to Scotsmen for exceptional service to the throne and candidates are personally selected by the monarch. When Queen Victoria came to the throne none of the sixteen Knights of the Thistle had a rank below Viscount, and they included one of the Queen's 'wicked uncles', HRH Prince Augustus Frederick, Duke of Sussex (1773–1843).

The thistle seems to have emerged as a Scottish emblem through a Danish invasion of Scotland. In the early days of organised war in Scotland it was considered unwarlike to attack an enemy at night. Danish invaders, however, decided to attack under the cover of darkness. To cloak their approach they moved on the unsuspecting Scots barefoot. One soldier stepped on a thistle, cried out, and alerted the Scots. In the ensuing battle the Danes were routed with great loss of life. Grateful Scots adopted the emblem thereafter as a symbol of their nation.

OFFICERS OF ARMS (SCOTLAND)

Lyon King of Arms

A GOLD CROWN composed of sixteen Acanthus leaves arising from a plain Gold circlet on which is inscribed in raised Roman Capitals: 'MISERERE MEI DEUS SECUNDUM MAGNAM TUAM MISERICORDIAM.'

A SILVER GILT SCEPTRE enamelled blue, powdered with Roses, Thistles, Trefoils, and Fleurs-de-lys, in Gold, and tipped at each end with Gold knobs on which are the Royal Arms.

The ENAMELLED BADGE of the Order of the Thistle suspended from a triple Gold chain.

A SILVER GILT COLLAR of SS.

The TABARD or the KING'S COAT of Velvet and Cloth of Gold embroidered with the Royal Arms, and a BLACK VELVET CAP embroidered with a Crowned Thistle Badge.

The THISTLE MANTLE, as described in the Statutes of the Order, only worn at ceremonies of the Order.

Collar of the Most Ancient and Most Noble Order of the Thistle, Scotland's own Order of Chivalry. The monarch is Sovereign of the Order and the Thistle is limited to sixteen knights; the Secretary of the Order is the Lord Lyon. The collar is gold with sixteen thistles each separated by four sprigs of rue. The badge worn with the collar shows a haloed St Andrew with his crux decussata (the Scottish Saltire) with the motto Nemo me impune lacessit *[Nobody attacks me with Impunity].*

Full Dress

COATEE. Scarlet Cloth, single-breasted, stand collar. The collar and cuffs of Blue-Black Velvet and pocket flaps of Scarlet Cloth on the waist seam. Nine buttons up the front showing between the embroidered edges (which are made to hook), two at the waist behind and two at the bottom of the back skirts. Gold embroidery on the edges, fronts, collar, cuffs, pocket flaps, back, skirts, back skirts and side edges. Scarlet Silk linings.

BUTTONS. Gilt, mounted, the Royal Cypher and Imperial Crown.

BREECHES: White kerseymere with knee buttons.

HOSE: White silk.

SHOES: Black patent leather.

BUCKLES: Gilt with Rose, Shamrock and Thistle motif.

SWORD: Black scabbard and gilt mountings.

SWORD KNOT: Gold lace strap with bullion tassel

SWORD BELT: White web, with white cloth frog.

HAT: Black beaver cocked hat, black silk cockade.

GLOVES. White.

Levée Dress

COATEE. Scarlet Cloth, single-breasted, stand collar, Blue-Black Velvet collar and cuffs, and pocket flaps of Scarlet Cloth. The collar, .cuffs, and pocket flaps and back embroidered in Gold. Three bands of Gold Lace, ⅜-inch wide, above cuffs. Nine buttons up the front (to button), and two at the waist behind, and two at the bottom of the back skirts. Scarlet Silk linings.

BUTTONS:
SWORD:
SWORD KNOT: } As for Full Dress.
HAT:

SWORD BELT. With Blue Cloth frog.

TROUSERS. Blue Cloth, with stripes of Gold Oakleaf lace on the side seams 2½ inches wide.

BOOTS. Plain Military, Patent Leather.

GREAT COAT. As for Household Uniform, buttons as for the Coatee.

James Francis Henry St Clair Erskine, 5th Earl of Rosslyn (1869–1939), in 1900, eccentric landowner, actor and writer. He earned international fame as 'The Man Who Broke The Bank At Monte Carlo'.

Prime Minister William Ewart Gladstone (1809–98) visits Glamis Castle, Angus, during the final days of his premiership, c. 1893. His host Claude, 13th Earl of Strathmore, is seated on the steps in front of Gladstone.

Pages of Honour, Scotland

The FROCK is of Green Poplin, and the HAT is trimmed with Green Feathering. In other respects, the dress is identical with that of a Page of Honour at the English Court.

Dress Worn at Court (Guide)

HIS MAJESTY'S LIEUTENANTS OF COUNTIES

New Regulations, War Office, 1908

COCKED HAT. Black Silk. On the right side, a Black Silk Cockade with a loop of Four Silver Bullions, the inner rows twisted, Silver Plated Button of the pattern worn on Coatee; Flat Gold Tassel, seven Gold Bullions with eleven Crimson Bullions under them.
PLUME. White Swan Feathers, drooping outwards, 10 inches long, with red feathers under them long enough to reach the end of the white ones; feathered stem 3 inches long.
COATEE.★ Scarlet Cloth. Double-breasted; Stand-up Collar, with rounded points; two rows of Buttons down the front, nine in each row, a space to be left between the eighth and ninth button for the waist belt, two at waist behind; the Skirts turned back with white, ¾ inch wide at the waist and about 2½ inches at the points. Collar and Cuffs of Blue Cloth. Scarlet Cloth Slashes on the Sleeves and Three Pointed Flaps at the Waist. The Collar, Flaps, Cuffs and Slashes trimmed with Silver Embroidery. Device in Embroidery, either a Rose, Prince of Wales's Plume, Thistle, or Shamrock at the point of the skirts. Body lined with White Silk and the skirts lined with White Cloth.
EPAULETTES. Silver. Device in Gold Embroidery, either the Rose, Prince of Wales's Plume, Thistle, or Shamrock, with Crown above.
EMBROIDERY. Silver. Oakleaf and Acorn for English and Welsh Counties, Thistle for Scotch Counties, and Shamrock for Irish Counties.
BUTTONS. Plated. Rose, Thistle, or Shamrock, with Crown above. For Welsh Counties the Prince of Wales's Plume.
GLOVES. White.

★His Majesty's Lieutenants who are Aide-de-Camp to the King will not wear their Military Aiguillettes with their Lieutenant's Uniform.

Dress Worn at Court (Guide)

Soldiers of the Atholl Highlanders parading at Blair Atholl, c. 1880. The regiment was raised by John Murray, 4th Duke of Atholl (1755–1830) as part of the British Army to fight in the American War of Independence. It was later disbanded, but reformed in 1839 and acted as bodyguard to Queen Victoria during her stay at Blair Castle in 1844. In 1845 colours were presented to the regiment on behalf of Queen Victoria by Lady Glenlyon, supported by two of Queen Victoria's daughters. The regiment forms the only recognised private army in Europe.

Mabell, Countess of Airlie (1866–1956), Lady-in-Waiting to Queen Mary, opens Dundee Flower Show on 29 August 1907, at Magdalen Green, in the presence of the monocled Lord Provost William Longair.

Court Dress (left) and Field Dress (right) of the Royal Bodyguard for Scotland, known as the Royal Company of Archers. Administered from Archers' Hall, Edinburgh, the Archers are a part of the Royal Household in Scotland and wear braided green doublets and Kilmarnock bonnets decorated with eagles' feathers. The Company of Archers was formally constituted in 1676 and continues ceremonial duties as well as undertaking bowmanship.

The 4th Earl of Mansfield (1806–98) surrounded by his family and friends at Scone Palace. Mansfield lunched with Queen Victoria during her first visit to Scotland in 1842, and became Lord Lieutenant of Clackmannanshire, becoming the longest and oldest serving royal officer in that position.

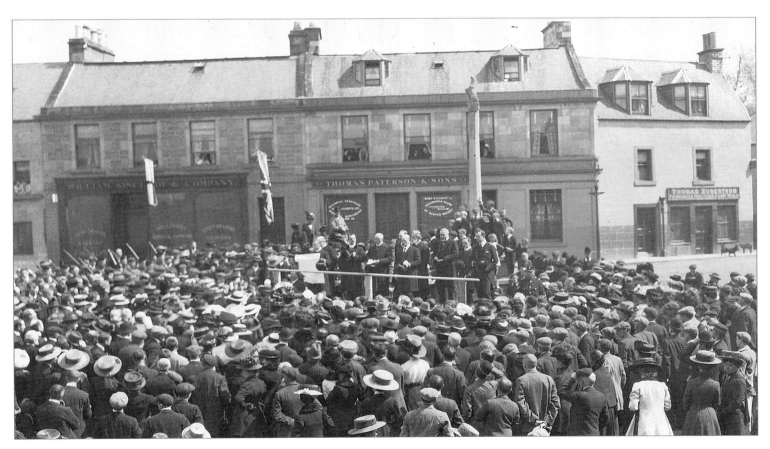

The Provost of Melrose reads the proclamation of George V at Melrose, 10 May 1910.

William Henry Walter, Earl of Dalkeith (later 6th Duke of Buccleuch and 8th Duke of Queensberry), his wife lady Louisa Jane Hamilton, Mistress of the Robes to Queen Victoria, and their two sons John Charles and George William, entertain a group of relatives at Langholm Lodge, East Dumfriesshire, 1879.

ECCENTRIC AYRSHIRE LAIRD

Another crack-brained laird in the same county has left inscribed on a stone monument upon his property a record of his eccentricity. I came upon it standing by itself near an oak tree at Todhills in the parish of Dalry. On the west side of the stone the following inscription has been cut:

> There is an oak tree a little from this, planted in the year 1761, it has 20 feet of ground round it for to grow upon, and all within that ground reserved from all succeeding proprietors for the space of 500 years from the above date by me, ANDREW SMITH, who is the offspring of many Andrew Smiths who lived in Auchengree for unknown generations.

On the south side the stone bears the sub-joined lines:

> My Trustees
> ROBERT GLASGOW
> Esq of
> Montgreenan
> WILLIAM COCHRAN
> Esq of
> Ladyland
> I stand here to herd this tree
> And if you please to read a wee
> In seventeen hundred and sixty one
> It was planted then at three feet long
> I'll tell more if you would ken
> It was planted at the byre end
> I'll tell you more you'll think a wonder
> It's alloud to stand for years five hundred
> It has twelve yards a cross and round about
> It belongs to no man till that time is out

> But to ANDREW SMITH tho he were dead
> He raised it out of the seed
> So cut it neither Top nor Tail
> Least that the same you do bewail
> Cut it neither Tail nor Top
> Least that some evil you oertak
> Erected
> By
> ANDREW SMITH
> of Todhills Octr 1817

When in the year 1867 the British Association met in Dundee, some of the members were entertained at Fingask – that charming old Scottish château, with its treasures of family and Jacobite antiquities. Among the visitors was Professor Charles Martin of Montpellier, who so delighted the Misses Murray Thriepland with his enthusiasm for Scotland and everything Scottish, that they bade him kneel, and taking a sword that had belonged to Prince Charlie, laid it on his shoulder and, as if the blade still possessed a royal virtue, dubbed him knight. Some years afterwards I chanced to meet him on a river steamer upon the Tiber, bound for Ostia with a party from the University of Rome. He was delighted to be addressed as 'Sir Charles Martin,' and recalled with evident enthusiasm the charms of Fingask and of the distinguished ladies who so hospitably entertained him there.

Sir Archibald Geikie

OLD SCOTS SCHOOLMASTERS

The Scottish schoolmaster of the old type is probably as extinct as the parish school system under which he flourished. What with revised codes, inspectors, examinations, grants in aid, Board of Education and other machinery, the educational arrangements of Scotland have during the last half-century been transformed to a remarkable degree. There can be no doubt that on the whole, and especially in recent years, the changes have been in the right direction. Nevertheless, we may regret the disappearance of some of the characteristic features of the old régime. The parish schools served to commingle the different classes of the community, and there was a freedom left to the teachers which gave them scope in their methods and range of subjects, and enabled them to send up to the university numbers of clever and well-trained scholars. Untrammelled by the fear of any school-board or Education Department, the 'dominie' was left to develop his own individuality, which, though it sometimes took the form of eccentricity, was in most cases the natural outgrowth of a cultivated mind, and was a distinct benefit to his pupils. In the delightful *Memories Grave and Gay* of Dr Kerr, who has spent his active life in practically furthering the cause of education in the country, an interesting account is given of the process of transformation, together with many anecdotes of his experience of country schools and country schoolmasters. To his ample stores those interested in the subject should turn.

'The Dominies', a 'Cabinet Portrait' of three old Scots schoolmasters by John Fergus of Largs, c. 1879. Along with doctors and clergymen, teachers were highly respected people, particularly in rural communities.

The Scots historian Dr David Hay Fleming (1849–1931), the son of a china merchant in St Andrews, became secretary of the Scottish History Society, and was an authority on Scotland's religious history. Victoria's reign saw the burgeoning of local history societies.

In the early days of examinations an inspector came to a school, and in the course of the reading stopped to ask the class the meaning of the word curfew in Gray's line: 'The curfew tolls the knell of parting day.' There was complete silence in the room. He tried to coax the boys on to an answer, but without effect; until the teacher, losing patience with them, exclaimed in vexation, 'Stupit fules! d'ye no ken what's a *whaup*?' whaup being *Scottice* for *curlew*.

A clerical friend of mine was, many years ago, visiting a parish school in Argyleshire where Gaelic was taught as well as English. He spoke to them in Gaelic, and asked them to spell one of the words he had used. They looked in blank amazement at him, and gave no reply. At last the master, turning round deprecatingly to the clergyman, said, 'Oich, sir, there's surely no spellin' in Gaelic.'

A story is told in the north of Scotland of a certain school in which a boy was reading in presence of an examiner, and on pronouncing the word *bull* as it is ordinarily sounded, was abruptly corrected by the schoolmaster.

'John, I've told you before, that word is called *bull*' (pronouncing it like *skull*).

'Excuse me, sir,' said the examiner, 'I think you will find that the boy has pronounced it correctly.'

'O no, sir, we always call it *bull* in this parish.'

'But you must pardon me if I say that the boy's pronunciation is the usual one. Have you a pronouncing dictionary?'

'Dictionary! O yes. Charlie, rin round to the house and fetch me the big dictionary. Meantime, John, go on wi' the reading.' So John went on with 'bull,' and Charlie brought the dictionary, which the master turned up in triumph, 'There, sir, is the word with the mark above the *u*, and there are the words that it's to be sounded like – put, push, pull (pronouncing these all like but, brush, dull). And now, John, you will go on wi' *bull*.'

Sir Archibald Geikie

CHARACTERFUL MINISTERS

No feature in the social changes which Scotland has undergone stands out more conspicuously than the part played in these changes by the clergy since the Reformation. This clerical influence has been both beneficial and baneful. On the one hand, the clergy have unquestionably taken a large share in the intellectual development of the people, and in giving to the national character some of its most distinctive qualities. For many generations, in face of a lukewarm or even hostile nobility and government, they bore the burden of the parish schools, elaborating and improving a system of instruction which made their country for a long time the best educated community in Europe. They have held up the example of a high moral standard, and have laboured with the most unremitting care to train their flocks in the paths of righteousness.

On the other hand, the clergy, having from the very beginning of Protestantism obtained control over the minds and consciences of the people, have naturally used this powerful influence to make their theological tenets prevail throughout the length and breadth of the land. They early developed a spirit of intolerance and fanaticism, and with this same spirit they succeeded in imbuing their people, repressing the natural and joyous impulses of humanity, and establishing an artificial and exacting code of conduct, the enforcement of which led to an altogether hurtful clerical domination. While waging war against older forms of superstition, they introduced new forms which added to the terrors and the gloom of life. These transformations were longest in reaching their climax among the Highlands and Islands, but have there attained the most complete development. Happily, in the Lowlands for the last two hundred years, their effects have been slowly passing away. The growth of tolerance and enlightenment is increasingly marked both among the clergy and the laity. But the old leaven is not even yet wholly eradicated, though it now works within a comparatively narrow and continually contracting sphere.

Dr Hanna relates that a Highland minister once went to baptise a child in the house of one of his parishioners, near which ran a small burn or river. When he came to the stream it was so swollen with recent rains that he could not ford it in order to reach the house. In these circumstances he told the father, who was awaiting him on the opposite bank, to bring the child down to the burn-side. Furnished with a wooden scoop, the clergyman stood on the one side of the water, and the father, holding the infant as far out in his arms as he could, placed himself on the other. With the foaming torrent between the participants, the service went on, until the time came for sprinkling the babe, when the minister, dipping the scoop into the water, flung its contents across the baby's face. His aim, however, was not good, for he failed more than once, calling out to the father after each new trial: 'Weel, has't gotten ony yet?' When he did succeed, the whole contents of the scoop fell on the child's face, whereupon the disgusted parent ejaculated, 'Ach, Got pless me, sir, but ye've trownt ta child.' Dr Chalmers, in telling this story, used to express his wonder as to what the great sticklers for form and ceremony in the sacraments would think of such a baptism by a burn-side, performed with a wooden scoop.

John Johnston, chauffeur to Dr Calder of Kirkhill, Coldingham, 1910. Medical practitioners and clergymen were among the first in Scotland to change from horse-drawn conveyances to motor vehicles.

A certain parish church in Carrick, like many ecclesiastical edifices of the time in Scotland, was not kept with scrupulous care. The windows seemed never to be cleaned, or indeed opened, for cobwebs hung across them, 'And half-starv'd spiders prey'd on half-starv'd flies.' There was an air of dusty neglect about the interior, and likewise a musty smell. One Sunday an elderly clergyman from another part of the country was preaching. In the midst of his sermon a spider, suspended from the roof at the end of its long thread, swung to and fro in front of his face. It came against his lips and was blown vigorously away. Again it swung back to his mouth, when, with an indignant motion of his hands, he broke the thread and exclaimed, 'My friends, this is the dirtiest kirk I ever preached in. I'm like to be pusioned wi' speeders.'

It is recorded of an old minister in the west of Ross-shire that he prayed for Queen Victoria, 'that God would bless her and that as now she had grown to be an old woman, He would be pleased to make her a new man.'

The same worthy divine is said to have once prayed 'that we may be saved from the horrors of war, as depicted in the pages of the *Illustrated London News* and the *Graphic*'

One of the most serious functions which the Presbyterian clergymen of Scotland had formerly to discharge was that of publicly examining their congregation in their knowledge of the Christian faith. Provided with a list of the congregation, the officiating minister in the pulpit proceeded to call up the members to answer questions out of the Shorter Catechism, or such other interrogatories as it might seem desirable to ask. Nobody knew when his turn would come, or what questions would be put to him, so that it was a time of trial and trepidation for old and young. The custom appears to be now obsolete, but reminiscences of its operation are still preserved.

Sir Archibald Geikie

A COUNTRY DOCTOR

A country doctor, who was attending a laird, had instructed the butler of the house in the art of taking and recording his master's temperature with a thermometer. On repairing to the house one morning he was met by the butler, to whom he said: 'Well, John, I hope the laird's temperature is not any higher to-day?' The man looked puzzled for a moment, and then replied: 'Weel, I was just wonderin' that mysell. Ye see he deed at twal' o'clock.' [Well, I was just wondering that myself. You see he died at twelve o'clock.]

A CLERGYMAN'S SON

A clergyman's son had taken to drink, and had given great trouble and pain to his worthy father. On one occasion, after a debauch of several days, he returned to the manse in the evening, and found that there had been a presbytery dinner in the house, and that the reverend fathers who had dined were now engaged over their toddy and talk in the study. He made for the room, and was immediately welcomed by his

Henderson's post office, Gavinton, Berwickshire, c. 1890. Post offices were key meeting places for local folk in rural nineteenth-century Scotland.

father, who tried to put the best face he could on the situation. He asked the young man where he had been. 'In hell,' was the answer. 'Ah, and what did you find there?' 'Much the same as I find here: I couldna see the fire for ministers.'

'IT MIGHT HAVE BEEN WORSE'

In a country parish in the west of Scotland the minister's man was a noted pessimist, whose only consolation to his friends in any calamity consisted in the remark, 'It micht hae been waur.' [It might have been worse.] One morning he was met by the minister, who told him he had had such a terrible dream that he had not yet been able to shake off the effects of it. 'I dreamt I was in hell, and experienced the torments of the lost. I never suffered such agony in my life, and even now I shudder when I think of it.' The beadle's usual consolatory remark came out, 'It micht hae been waur.' 'Oh John, John, I tell you it was the greatest mental distress I ever suffered in my life. How could it have been worse?' 'It micht hae been true,' was the reply.

RELIGIOUS MANIA

Cases of religious mania have been common enough in Scotland, where questions of theology have for centuries been keenly debated among all classes of the community. It has been said that 'the worst of madmen is a saint run mad'. Nevertheless, even those who have least sympathy with the theological tenets and ecclesiastical system of the Scottish clergy must needs acknowledge that, as earnest and indefatigable workers for the spiritual and temporal good of their flocks, as leaders in every movement for the benefit of the community, and as fathers of families, these men deserve the ample commendation which they have received. Their limited stipends have allowed them but a slender share of the material comforts and luxuries of life, and comparatively few of them have enjoyed opportunities to 'augment their small peculiar,' yet they have, as a whole, set a noble example of self-denial, thrift, and benevolence. Secure at least of their manses, they have contrived 'to live on with a cheerful heart,' respected and esteemed of men. While supplying the material wants of their people, as far as their means would allow, they have yet been able to provide a good education for their families, and to

> Put forth their sons to seek preferment out;
> Some to the wars, to try their fortune there;
> Some to discover islands far away;
> Some to the studious universities.

The 'sons of the manse' are found filling positions of eminence in every walk of life.

Sir Alexander Geikie

THE COST OF MEETING THE PEOPLE

A tour in Scotland will cost the traveller an average of £1 a day, even with care. But everywhere he will find hotels comfortable enough, at a general charge of from 3s 6d a bedroom, 4s *table d'hôte* dinner, 1s 6d attendance, 2s 6d breakfast, 2s simple lunch of cold meat and cheese. Added to this the ridiculous cost of baths (1s and 1s 6d) in bathrooms. It is a new feature in the books that in the case of hotels offering fishing and other attractions, where visitors are likely to stay some time, the terms for weekly board are given whenever possible. All prices mentioned are those for the season, unless otherwise stated. Some care has been taken to distinguish between the different kinds of hotels. Those recognisedly the largest and most important are placed first on the list, but those tested by personal experience and found really good of their kind, whatever the size may be, are starred. Their number is necessarily limited, and the fact of an hotel's not being starred is no indication that it may not be good also. The word pleasant is used to designate extra obligingness and civility, what may be called good humour, on the part of the host, for though courtesy of a kind is generally recognised by hotel-keepers to be essential to their business, there is not always the natural good humour, which saves so much friction.

Black's Guide to Scotland (1906)

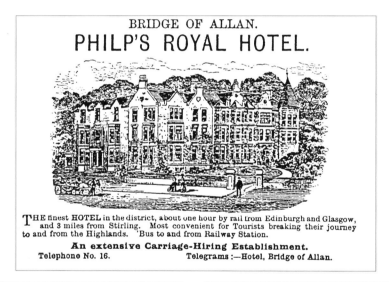

BRIDGE OF ALLAN.
PHILP'S ROYAL HOTEL.

THE finest HOTEL in the district, about one hour by rail from Edinburgh and Glasgow, and 3 miles from Stirling. Most convenient for Tourists breaking their journey to and from the Highlands. 'Bus to and from Railway Station.

An extensive Carriage-Hiring Establishment.

Telephone No. 16.   Telegrams :—Hotel, Bridge of Allan.

INNELLAN.
On the beautiful Firth of Clyde, between Dunoon and Rothesay.
NEW ROYAL HOTEL.

Rebuilt and opened May 1906.

WINDSOR HOTEL, GLASGOW.
PATRONISED BY ROYALTY.

First-Class Family Hotel. Central Position without noise of Traffic. Every Comfort. Electric Light. Passenger Elevator. Excellent Cuisine. A. M. THIEM, Proprietor.

Bank staff at 191 Ingram Street, Glasgow, branch of the Union Bank of Scotland (opened 1832). An early calculating machine and typewriter are features of the office.

THE SCOTTISH POUND NOTE: SYMBOL OF THE PEOPLE

The Scottish pound note has always been looked upon as a symbol of Scotland's financial independence. Banknote production in Scotland is undoubtedly part of a unique heritage, for the nation's paper currency has played a role of exceptional importance in Scotland's economic development. At their very basic cultural value, Scottish banknotes are wonderful examples of miniature graphic art. In particular, the steel engravings of Victorian issues show an uncommonly high standard of artwork and furthermore, Scottish paper money has an unequalled history in the chronicles of the world's banknotes.

Notes for 20s were first issued in Scotland in 1696 by the Bank of Scotland (founded in 1695) to meet the needs of small money transactions. Collector purists still argue that these notes were not true one pound notes as they were for 20s Scots and were thus only equal to 1s 8d sterling. The notes bore the calligraphy for 20s sterling, but to be equivalent to English currency they should have been marked for £12 sterling. This printing custom persisted until Scots money was discontinued in 1707, and as the Bank of England did not issue £1 notes until 1797, it can be said with some justification that the Scots invented the pound note. The Scottish note marked £1 was first issued by the Bank of Scotland on 7 April 1704. The earliest Scottish £1 note known to be in existence is the one of 16

April 1716 made out in favour of one David Spence and signed by that ardent supporter of the Jacobite cause, the banker David Drummond. The note is thought to have been printed on a tailledouce (copper-plate) printing press on paper that originated in France or the Netherlands.

When the notes were first issued they were treated with some suspicion, and towards the end of 1704, when there was a run on the notes, people clamoured at the banks to change their notes into silver. There were further runs on the Scottish pound note in 1715 when the Jacobites seized the issuing bank, and during the Napoleonic wars in the late eighteenth century. During periods when change was scarce among traders the banks allowed the £1 notes to be cut into halves or quarters to assist commerce. What made the Scottish pound note different from the English notes was that although the banknote was the main medium of exchange in Scotland, it was not so in England. Until 1793 the Bank of England had no notes of lower value than £10. Only during the First World War did the pound note become a permanent small note in England.

So popular did the £1 note become all over Scotland that many of the myriad small provincial banks issued their own. In 1825 the agent for the Commercial Bank at Wick, Caithness, reported to his employers that fishermen, farm labourers, coopers and housewives were strong supporters of the banknote and insisted on being paid with them. Cattle-drovers and horse-dealers too, were strong

No. 7 Bankers Company, Queen's Rifle Volunteer Brigade, The Royal Scots, 1905. This was the year of the Royal Review.

Bank of Scotland Rifle Club, 1897. The photograph was taken to commemorate Queen Victoria's Diamond Jubilee.

The National Bank of Scotland £1 note features the Marquess of Lothian, Governor of the Bank, alongside Edinburgh Castle.

The British Linen Bank, £1 note, 1911. Incorporated by Royal Charter in 1746, the bank kept up the high standard of engraving of the period.

supporters of the pound note, and at cattle fairs from Falkirk to Galashiels dealers could be identified by the bulging top pockets of their jackets where the notes were kept.

Demand for the £1 note increased every year and by 1825, thirty-two banks in Scotland had issued their own. The proposal of the English government, led by the Earl of Liverpool, to withdraw the Scottish £1 note caused public uproar, the suggestion being taken as a personal slight by every Scot. If the English had financial problems, why should Scotland suffer? Correspondence on the subject filled every newspaper, protest meetings were held all over the country, and parliament was inundated with petitions and remonstrances.

The feelings of the people were brought into fine focus by Sir Walter Scott, who contributed letters on the subject under the title 'Sir Malachi Malagrowther on the Proposed Changes of Currency', published in February–March 1826 and addressed to his old friend James Ballantyne, editor of the Edinburgh Evening Journal. English MPs declared Sir Walter Scott's letters to be an incitement to violence. William Croker, Secretary to the Admiralty, replied for the English authorities to counter Sir Walter Scott's attack. But Scott's romantic style and allusions to Scotland's traditions set 'the heather . . . on fire far and wide'. Sir Walter had tapped a rich vein of national sentiment and stirred up the latent resentment that had bubbled below the surface in Scotland since the largely unpopular Union of the parliaments of England and Scotland in 1707.

Thomas Kinneir, a director of the Bank of Scotland, warned Lord Liverpool that if the Scottish £1 note was withdrawn riots would break out, particularly in the agricultural communities. He was supported by the Duke of Argyll's factor, Lt-Col. Donald Campbell, who had witnessed groups of agricultural workers declaring their willingness to fight. The English government backed off, but in 1826 they passed an Act prohibiting the printing of notes under £5 in England. No Scottish notes were usable in England after 1829, and the Scottish notes were never legal tender.

The Commercial Bank of Scotland, £1 note, 1908. Apart from temporary provisions in both world wars, Scottish banknotes have never been legal tender, but they are legal currency.

The Town and County bank, £1 note, Aberdeen, 1903. Some of Scotland's 'small bank' banknotes survived into the 1940s.

Officers of the 7th Battalion, the Black Watch, at Binnend camp, 1913.

GOD-FEARING MERCHANTS

Glasgow merchants were rich men in those days but all of
them, without exception, lived in fear of what the future
might hold. And with reason, for scarcely a month passed in
which somebody did not disappear. That process was called
'going down the drain', and the description is apt. Town
house and country house, carriage and servants vanished in a
night, and the shorn sheep were left to face as best they
might a blast the bitterness of which was untempered.
Nothing was spared them; if the wretched bankrupt
happened to hold office in his Church he was compelled,
immediately, to offer his resignation, since default was
incompatible with Godliness in its more exalted exercise.

As a rule the family left the neighbourhood, and so were
able to join some other, and less important, congregation.
These 'mission churches', as they were called, were full of the
wreckage of the exchanges. One of them, I remember, was
associated with a wealthy congregation over which a famous
divine named Dr Edie presided. Dr Edie's church was in
Kelvinside, the 'mission church' was hidden in the gloom of
Cambridge Street. One Sunday morning a wag pinned the
following lines to the rich man's church door:

*At the heart of Aberdeen's civic pride lay the Municipal Buildings at
the eastern end of Union Street. These imposing buildings were
erected between 1868 and 1874 at the cost of £100,000.*

*Junction of Union Street and Justice Street, Aberdeen, featuring the City Cross (renovated 1842), and the statue of the 5th Duke of Gordon
(d. 1836); he was the last of the line of 'ancient Dukes'.*

This church is not for the poor and needy,
But for the rich and Doctor Edie.
The rich step in and take a seat;
The poor pass on to Cambridge Street.

There was no appeal. Even the terraces and crescents of the West End were numbered and ticketed so that a man's social status might be accurately and instantly known from his address. The best neighbourhood was that which looks down upon the West End Park. Kelvinside came next with its Atholl Gardens and Windsor Terrace and Westbourne Gardens. Indeed, the only people who might live in less expensive neighbourhoods without loss of caste, were ministers and doctors.

Ministers formed a class all by themselves, and were a constant source of interest and discussion. Everybody sat 'under' one or other of them, and it was a point of honour to uphold your choice as the finest preacher in the country. The sermons were long and, usually, insufferably tedious. So much so, indeed, that the jokes fired off at Church social gatherings were often, in reality, back-handers at the minister.

R. McNair Wilson, *Doctor's Progress* (1932)

CHAMPAGNE NOT SHERRY

Those were wonderful [Edwardian] days. Taxation and the cost of living were low; money was freely spent and wealth was everywhere in evidence. Moreover it was possessed largely by the nicest people, who entertained both in town and in the country. Dinners were gargantuan affairs, far too long, but although there were innumerable courses, the foreign fashion of serving innumerable wines had disappeared. It was very seldom that sherry was even offered with the soup. Champagne, port and old brandy were the order of the day, or rather, night.

George Cornwallis-West, *Edwardian Hey-Days* (1930)

UNLADYLIKE TO BE IN LOVE

Women are not like men, they cannot chuse, nor is it creditable or ladylike to be what is called in love; I believe that few . . . well-regulated minds ever have been and that romantic attachment is confined to novels and novel-readers, ye silly and numerous class of young persons ill-educated at home or brought up at boarding-schools.

Mary Glynn, quoting her aunt (*c.* 1890)

Marriage was fundamental to Scottish society one hundred years ago, and imperative for the non-intellectual, or non-aristocratic woman if she were to have any position in society. Here at Edinchip, Lochearnhead, Margaret Helen MacGregor (daughter of Rear-Admiral Sir Malcolm MacGregor of MacGregor, Chief of the Clan Gregor) poses with her new husband The Hon. Alan David Murray, later 6th Earl of Mansfield, 20 April 1899.

A PROPOSAL AND HOME AFTER THE HONEYMOON

Contrary to our expectations we shall always all look back to this . . . ball with very great pleasure. We did not know many people there but after a short time Lord Carrington arrived, danced with me, & then something took place which has made me *very, very* happy. I went to mother & whispered in her ear 'I have won the jacket' (one that Mother worked & put aside for the first one of her girls who married). I ought indeed to be grateful for this great happiness, & I *am*. There is no one like him . . . Father & Mother are *very* fond of him. . . .

The whole town was decorated, every balcony & window was full of people & there were 3 beautiful Arches. After 4 Addresses had been given & Charlie [Lord Carrington] had answered two, the horses were taken out of the carriage (the phaeton) & the Fire Brigade pulled us all through the town and up to our door. I shall never forget our reception, there were thousands of people! We fed 300,000 [*sic*] children in the park etc. After dinner we went out . . . to see a large bonfire & then on to the balcony of some old people called Grove. Directly we came out . . . we were known. It was a heavenly night.

Lady Carrington, *Diary* (1878)

MARRIAGE FOR MONEY

When I grew up, society was expanding and becoming more moneyed, and a less rural standard was creeping in. Society, so called, had also become much larger. Some eldest sons of peers married Americans and other heiresses, which buttressed family fortunes at the cost of bringing in much higher standards of smartness in clothes and equipages.

Susan Tweedsmuir, *The Lilac and the Rose* (1952)

MARRIAGE SETTLEMENTS

The business side of [such] arrangements was shrouded under a sacred cloth of tradition and accepted formality, and solicitors were usually left to deal with the legal intricacies. Contributions towards a couple's maintenance and provisions for offspring of the marriage came from the two families involved. The contribution from the wife's family was known as the dowry, or portion, and this was settled on the couple, though the husband usually held control of it, and the wife was allowed a small sum known as pin money.

Maureen E. Montgomery, *Gilded Prostitution, 1870–1914*

BOSSY MOTHERS-IN-LAW

Widowed mothers, from Windsor Castle to the humblest cottage, exacted obedience from sons and daughters, no matter what their age. A son's wife was as much subject to her mother-in-law in Britain as she would have been in India.

The characterful 'Coal Jean' and 'Coal Geordie' of Peebles, 1880. They followed the coal delivery carts and offered their services as coal heavers to customers who had just had loose coal dumped at their doors.

My husband's mother [Blanche, Dowager Lady Airlie] had her own house in London, but she – and all her children – regarded Cortachy [Castle, Angus] as her home. Her every wish was law there. The servants were hers and perfectly trained by her. I had no scope for my own initiative. My position as the wife of the head of the family was not recognised.

Mabell, Countess of Airlie, *Thatched with Gold* (1962)

DUNDEE LADIES OF THE NIGHT

The social evil was then pretty pronounced. Big-breasted, sturdy, short-petticoated strumpets walked about the streets quite unashamed, and the language heard in such avenues as the Overgate on a Saturday night was quite appalling. One of the most notorious of these bold women was a giant negress known as 'Black Mag'. She sailed away to Melbourne one day the wife of the second mate of a Yankee craft (a darky), laden with pavements, flooring, and baled goods. What a deliverance to the town, what a curse to that fated vessel!

Sir John Fleming, *Looking Backwards for Seventy Years* (1922)

Street musicians like Albert Wallace of Selkirk were a common sight in Scotland a hundred years ago. Wallace was nicknamed 'The Border Minstrel'.

BEGGARS MAKE GOOD ACTORS

There were, of course, some characters about in my younger days not easy to forget. One, a young fellow, Stobie by name, [was] known as 'Stobie the thief'. He was continually in prison for all sorts of thefts. He had a most repellent look, high cheek-bones, and deep sunken eyes and a sly slinking way with him. We boys ran away when we saw him coming. Strange to say, he married in after years, and for some time led a reformed life, but after a time broke out again in his old ways and disappeared from view.

Another was 'Blind Hughie', an almost blind middle-aged man with a strong baritone voice, who had quite a stock of Scotch songs, which he sang excellently. Hughie led a decent life, and supported his wife and family respectably. He sang also on the streets of many other towns, from Edinburgh to Aberdeen.

The flax spinner, Perthshire, c. 1890. Coarse linen made from the locally grown blue-flowered flax plant was a common cottage industry in Scotland.

Another rather repulsive character was a sturdy young beggar fellow, who for a time plied his trade lucratively by soliciting alms and, if refused, bursting into tears, and if still refused, falling down into convulsive fits, which he could bring on at any time. Becoming a nuisance, he was taken to the Poorhouse.

Another character lived opposite to us, a publican named Sandy Deans, who kept what was known as the Bannockburn Tavern, which had a large canvas displayed above the door, depicting a battle scene with Bruce in front with drawn sword.

Sir John Fleming

THE TONE-DEAF DOWAGER

My first visit to the opera had been many years previously, when I was invited to the box of the old Duchess of Montrose by a girl friend who was a relation of hers. The first thing the old lady asked me when I arrived was: 'Do you like music, young man?' I said I did. 'I don't,' she answered – 'at any rate, not this!' and promptly went to sleep.

George Cornwallis-West

IF IT WASN'T FOR THE WEAVERS

Some folks are independent o' ther tradesmen's *wark*, [work]
For women need *nae* Barber, an' dykers need nae Clerk; [no]
But they *canna* do without a coat or a sark,   [cannot]
Na! they canna want the wark o' the Weavers.
If it *warna* the weaver what wad we do?   [was not]
 We *wadna* get *claith* made o' our *woo'*,   [would not/cloth/wool]
We wadna get a coat neither black nor blue,
 Gin't warna for the wark o' the Weavers.   [If it were not]

Traditional Ballad

THE CLOTH TRADE

Let us in imagination go back sixty or seventy years ago, and peep into the little window of a weaver's shop – the walls of which are adorned with quaint prints and ballads, bought from time to time for handfuls of 'thrums' from the vendor or singer of this class of literature. Our desire is to witness the operation of beginning a new web. We find that when the web was put on the beam several fellow-craftsmen required to be present to give a helping hand. This was called beaming the web. It was done in this way. The chain of yarn was laid on a clean cloth on the floor. The end of it was then thrown over a pole above the loom, and brought back over what was called a 'niffler' which was held by two persons to spread the yarn over the beam. They drove the beam round by means of a handle fixed in a hole of the beam. The man who sat at the chain of yarn held it firmly in his hands. The end of the chain was fixed on a rod which was placed in a groove in the beam. The winding of the chain then began. When it was rolled the beam was placed on the top of the loom, and the ends were allowed to hang down like a fringe. A boy or a girl sat on the outside of what was called the 'caums', and handed thread after thread to the weaver on the other side, who took it between his fingers and drew it through the 'caums'. This was called, on the boy's part, 'gi'en in the web', and on the weaver's part, 'takin' in the web.'

The web having been 'gi'en in', the weaver placed each of the threads into the reed by means of a little instrument styled a slae-hook. This finished, the reed was put into the lathe, and the ends of the yarn tied to a rod fixed to the breast-beam. The work was now ready for the shuttle, whose duty it was to drag through the woof. The treadles were operated on by the feet to work the 'caums', and by this means a roadway or shed was made in the threads, through which the shuttle ran in its groove of the lathe. The reed in the lathe was then brought firmly up on the thread or woof, and so the cloth was formed. The shuttle was driven by a handle fixed to cords that were attached to the driver which ran on spindles. The shuttle turned at the end of the groove, and was driven to the other side. The weaver sat on a seat which moved on pins placed in rests on each side of the loom. This seat moved as his feet went up and down on the treadles, which were laid in a hole made in the floor. The web of cloth as it proceeded was rolled up on a beam immediately above the treadles, near the knees of the

A broad handframe and winding wheel being worked at John Laing & Son's hosiery mill, Hawick, c. 1910.

worker, and this was called the cloth beam. Every now and then the yarn was rolled off the beam to the extent of two or three yards, and dressed with flour paste, which was spread on two hair brushes, and drawn above and below the yarn. When the paste dried another brush smeared with tallow was drawn over the yarn to make it slide easily through the 'caums'.

In former days the yarns woven on the hand loom were generally hand spun. The country guidwife perhaps bought a mat of flax, or she would grow and dress her own flax. A 'stent' of yarn was spun each day, and she sold her yarns, just as she sold her butter and eggs, in the town. Even in towns, the servant girls had each their daily amount of spinning, but in such cases the flax was got from the manufacturers. Almost every little grocery shop had on its window shutter the intimation – 'Lint and Tow given out to spin.' On most of the holdings around the muir a considerable quantity of flax was grown and prepared for the weaver, and evidence of the presence of lint pots is still to be seen in a number of fields. The flax grown in the district required to be 'skutched', or cleaned of the fibre, for which process there were a number of mills along the banks of the Lunan, and thus home flax, as well as that which was imported, required to be dressed, or 'heckled' before being spun.

The pirn wheel was to be seen at work in every weaver's home, either by the side of his loom, or 'ben the hoose' in the kitchen and living room. The wife had to fill her husband's pirns, and even the young folks had, after school hours, to wind their 'stent' before they got their supper. For the benefit

of some of our readers it would perhaps be necessary to explain that the pirn (or reel) wheel wound the weft from the 'whisks' on the pirns attached to a spindle, which was driven by means of a belt of cat-gut round the wheel. When a pirn was filled it was placed into a box or basket, which, when full was handed to the weaver. It is hardly necessary to add that when four looms were at work together in a small, low-roofed 'shop', and a pirn wheel was buzzing in their midst like a great bee, the scene was one of such noise and stern hard work that a visitor could not hear himself speak.

The spinning wheel has gone from our rural districts, only a worm-eaten relic can be found in a day's tramp.

D.H. Edwards, *Glimpses of Men and Manners* (1920)

THE LADY'S MAID

What Swift and Defoe thought of the lady's maid we already know. Dramatists and novelists showed her as a vain, twittering, tongue-poking baggage, with morals hardly any better than those of her mistress. In *The Rivals*, Lucy is made to say: 'Let girls in my station be as fond as they please of appearing expert and knowing in their trusts; commend me to a mask of *silliness* and a pair of sharp eyes for my own interest under it.' Lower servants generally disliked the lady's maid, partly because of her affectations and pertness, partly because she stood too close to her mistress's ear, partly because a housemaid knew her chances of promotion to lady's maid were slim. The governess also disliked the lady's maid and the enmity was returned; each was jealous of the other's standing.

The specifications for a good lady's maid were exacting. Firstly, she had to be willing to perform for another woman those intimate services which nine women out of ten are modest enough to wish to do for themselves. She had to be young, reasonably tall, discreet, cheerful, submissive; healthy enough to withstand long hours; considerate enough not to fall asleep on her mistress in the carriage; virtuous enough to withstand footmen; honest enough to look after jewels; tolerant enough not to resent the master's untidy, time-wasting incursions into feminine territory; educated well enough to read to her mistress and not to go looking for 'a coarse dish with a handle' when asked for Corfe's edition of

Handel. She was expected to have a near-expert knowledge of hairdressing and to be unusually skilled at needlework; and she was even supposed to have a flair for practical chemistry. In token of her superior status she usually had her own carpeted room which the other servants were not suffered to enter, except to clean the floor and carry away the slops. She took her meals in the housekeeper's room. A superior lady's maid would work for one lady only and any request to attend two or more would precipitate the sort of trouble which occurred in *The Admirable Crichton*. In a pretentious household, even a child of seven or eight might have her own maid, but in less wealthy establishments one lady's maid would be expected to look after two, or even three, daughters.

The most vivacious ladies' maids were French, but they had their inbuilt disadvantages, not least at times of international crisis. In the invasion scare of 1803 Lady Elizabeth Foster, later Duchess of Devonshire, was called to the Aliens Office to justify her employment of French maids at Devonshire House and had to put up quite a spirited fight to retain them. For the average middle-class mistress, French maids set too fast a pace. 'A Parisian maid out of her orbit is not a treasure,' wrote an authority of the later Victorian years. 'In her orbit, as attendant to an extravagant, wealthy and fashionable mistress, she suits the post and what is no less important, the post suits her.' It was impossible to inquire too carefully into the character of French ladies' maids, according to this writer. Less troublesome, more solid, more trustworthy were Swiss maids; but they lacked vivacity.

In essence the duty of the lady's maid was to dress, undress and re-dress her mistress as often as the day's commitments required. Rising early, she ensured that the housemaid had lit the fire in her mistress's dressing-room. She then called her mistress, told her the time, laid out her clothes, carried in the hot water and went for breakfast. When the bell rang she would attend her mistress in the dressing-room, comb her hair and wait on her until she was dressed, afterwards tidying up the bedroom and dressing-room. She then retired to her room or the housekeeper's room to sew or iron, unless she was required to walk out with her mistress, or alone with a pet dog. After lunch she once more attended her mistress, dressing her for her afternoon outing, tidied up again and continued with her sewing or other chores until her employer returned to be undressed and dressed again for dinner. After that she had little or nothing to do until her mistress rang the bell to be undressed for bed, except to see that the maids kept up the bedroom fire and to lay out a nightdress in front of it. If her mistress kept late hours, the lady's maid would not expect to go to bed until three or four in the morning.

E.S. Turner, *What the Butler Saw* (1962)

THE WORLD OF THE TINKERS

ON the roads of the north of Scotland, any time after the last snow-wreaths have melted behind the dykes, you will meet a

Maids drawing water at the well in the courtyard of Earlshall, Fife. Ladies' maids, parlour maids, kitchen maids and scullery maids were all essential employees in the wealthy Scots household a hundred years ago. Ladies' maids were great sources of household gossip and scandal.

The head gardener and his staff of twenty-two at The Hirsel Estate, Coldstream, Berwickshire, 1870. Such photographs of servants with the tools of their trade are rare.

The head gardener instructs his staff at The Hirsel, 1880. The well-to-do espoused the habit of 'pottering' in their gardens while the servants did all the back-breaking tasks. In The Forsyte Saga *John Galsworthy mentions the vogue of employing 'Scotch gardeners' as the most hardworking.*

peculiar kind of tinker. They are not the copper-nosed scarecrows of the lowlands, sullen and cringing, attended by sad infants in ramshackle perambulators. Nor are they in any sense gipsies, for they have not the Romany speech or colouring. They travel the roads with an establishment, usually a covered cart and one or more lean horses, and you may find their encampments any day by any burnside. Of a rainy night you can see their queer little tents, shaped like a segment of sausage, with a fire hissing at the door, and the horse cropping the roadside grass; of a fine morning the women will be washing their duds on the loch shore and their young fighting like ferrets among the shingle. You will meet with them in the back streets of the little towns, and at the back doors of wayside inns, but mostly in sheltered hollows of the moor or green nooks among the birches, for they are artists in choosing camping-grounds. They are children of Esau who combine a dozen crafts – tinkering, fish-hawking, besom-making, and the like – with their natural trades of horse-coping and poaching. At once brazen and obsequious, they beg rather as an art than a necessity; they will whine to a keeper with pockets full of pheasants' eggs, and seek permission to camp from a laird with a melting tale of hardships, while one of his salmon lies hidden in the bracken on their cart floor. The men are an upstanding race, keen-eyed, resourceful, with humour in their cunning; the women, till life bears too hardly on them, are handsome and soft-spoken; and the children are burned and weathered like

imps of the desert. Their speech is neither lowland nor highland, but a sing-song Scots of their own, and if they show the Celt in their secret ways there is a hint of Norse blood in the tawny hair and blue eyes so common among them.

John Buchan, *John Macnab* (1925)

Some tinkers camped in groups, others in family units. By and large they considered themselves independent of society and its expectations. Schooling was usually considered valueless except for rudimentary reading and writing skills, so tinker children had little education, although they seem to have been kindly treated within their own groups. Here the Maclaren family are pictured at their camp in Angus just before the turn of the century.

Chapter 5

THE CULT OF ROBERT BURNS

*T*he Victorian Age was to see a great spawning of memorabilia concerning the Scots poet Robert Burns (1759–96). Its momentum gradually built up from the summer of 1844 when a great festival was sponsored at Alloway, Ayrshire – Burns's birthplace – to honour his surviving sons. As early as 1815 an elegant mausoleum in Burns's memory had been raised at St Michael's churchyard, Dumfries – the town where Burns died – and as the nineteenth century progressed a myriad panels, plaques, roundells and statues appeared all over Scotland to pay homage to the Bard. The Burns National Monument was erected in Edinburgh in 1830, although the statue to Burns was not set up in Glasgow's George Square until 1877.

Souvenirs of the Bard were to be found everywhere in nineteenth-century Scotland; they ranged from artifacts purporting to have belonged either to Burns himself or his friends, to objects made from materials found on the sites of Burns's activities. Among the many souvenirs displayed at the Centenary Exhibition at Glasgow in 1896 one of the earliest was a piece of yew from Crookston Castle (Midlothian), upon which Burns had carved his name. At the Palace of Holyroodhouse, Edinburgh, is still displayed the chair (built from rafter wood taken from Alloway Kirk by John Underwood in 1822), depicting scenes from Burns's famous poem 'Tam O'Shanter' (1790); this chair was later acquired by Queen Victoria.

During Victoria's widowhood at Balmoral, she was read to from the works of Burns by the jovial, larger-than-life Presbyterian

Postcard views of places associated with Robert Burns (1759–96), with his image superimposed, began to be popular in the 1890s.

Jean Armour Burns Brown (1864–1937) great-granddaughter of Robert Burns, was much sought out at her home at Dumfries by Burns devotees, particularly as she bore a striking resemblance to her famous ancestor.

minister, the Revd Dr Norman Macleod (1812–72), her favourite preacher at nearby Crathie Church.

There was a brisk trade too, in postcards associated with Burns from around the 1870s. Especially collectible were pictures of his wife Jean Armour and his beloved Agnes Maclehose (his literary 'Clarinda'), the survivors among his nine offspring, his recognised illegitimate children and their mothers, and his descendants, including Jean Armour Burns Brown (1864–1937), the poet's great-granddaughter.

The Burns Federation was established in 1885. Among its other purposes, it was intended to encourage Burns Clubs (and kindred societies), to keep the 'Old Scots Tongue' alive, and to stimulate the development of Scottish literature, art and music. Although several Burns enthusiasts used to meet in a haphazard way to preserve his memory from as early as the late 1700s, the first proper club was the Greenock Burns Club, consolidated on 21 July 1801. Thereafter clubs proliferated, particularly during the period from 1886 to 1918.

During the Victorian and Edwardian years there appeared a great number of volumes of engravings of places which local traditions averred inspired Robert Burns's work, and no Scottish household was complete without a copy of his works. The Kilmarnock Edition of his poems had appeared on 31 July 1786; this was followed by the Edinburgh Edition on 21 April 1787.

BURNS AND HIS LOVE OF BOOKS

THE diffusion of knowledge was a favourite object with Burns. For this he established his reading and debating clubs in the west, and in the same spirit he desired to excite a love of literature among the peasants of Dunscore. He undertook the management of a small parochial library, and wrote out the rules. Mr Riddell, of Friars-Carse, and other gentlemen, contributed money and books. The library commenced briskly, but soon languished. The poet could not always be

John Masey Wright's (1777–1866) stylised picture of Burns with barmaid Elizabeth Paton, who bore him an illegitimate daughter, Elizabeth (1784–1817: 'Dear bought Bess').

Thou's welcome, *wean. Mishanter fa*' me,   [child/mishap/befall]
If thought o' thee, or yet thy mammie,
Shall ever daunton me or awe me
My sweet, wee lady,
Or if I blush when thou shalt ca' me
tyta or daddie.

The Masons' Walk, Tarbolton, from St James's Lodge, by David Octavius Hill (1802–70) and Thomas Higham (1796–1844). Burns moved into Lochlea Farm, Tarbolton, Ayrshire, in 1771. He cynically lampooned the girls of the town in his 'The Tarbolton Lasses', but honoured the town's masons in his 'Farewell to the Brethren of St James's Lodge'.

present at the meetings; the subscribers lived far apart; disputes and disunion crept in, and it died away like a flower which fades for want of watering. Burns alludes ironically to the scheme in one of his letters. 'Wisdom,' he averred, 'might be gained by the mere handling of books.' His letters to the booksellers on the subject of this subscription library do him much honour; his choice of authors, which business was actually left to his discretion, being in the highest degree judicious.

Such institutions are now common, indeed almost universal, in the rural districts of Southern Scotland, but it should never be forgotten that Burns was among the first, if not the very first, to set the example. 'He was so good,' says Mr Riddell, 'as to take the whole management of this concern; he was treasurer, librarian, and censor, to our little society, which will long have a grateful sense of his public spirit and exertions for its improvement and information.'

John D. Ross *A Little Book of Burns Lore* (1926)

ROBERT BURNS: MASON

Robert Burns arrived in Edinburgh on Tuesday, 28th November 1786, and took up his abode in a sleeping apartment of Mrs Carfrae's lodgings, Baxter's Close, Lawnmarket, occupied by John Richmond, then a law-student and clerk from Mauchline. On that day one of his patrons, William Wallace, Advocate, Sheriff of Ayrshire, Professor of Scots Law in the university, and one of the assessors of the city of Edinburgh, died suddenly.

It was announced in the papers that a daylight procession of the Grand Lodge and lodges of the city would take place on the 30th, and brethren from the country were invited to join. On the 30th they assembled in the New Church aisle, and walked to St Andrew's Church, New Town, where the minister of Maybole, Ayrshire, author of a publication called 'Brotherly Love', addressed them. On the 6th December, Burns attended a judicial sale in the Parliament House of some lands in the parish of Tarbolton, for the information of his correspondent, Mr Hamilton . . . A meeting of the Canongate Kilwinning Lodge

Robert Burns in Masonic Dress as Deputy Master of the St James Tarbolton Kilwinning Masonic Lodge, No. 178. This unique portrait of Burns was prepared by P.E. Green and J.H. Thoms of Dundee in 1921.

Facsimile of Dumbarton Burgess Ticket, presented to Burns in 1787. It conferred on him the freedom of the town. In the nineteenth century documents and books associated with Burns were much collected. Most homes in Scotland, even the poorest, had two books: the Bible and the Works of Burns.

was advertised for the 7th, at half-past six in the evening; and, by Mr Dalrymple of Orangefield, a masonic brother of Burns, he was introduced to the Past-Master, the Hon. Henry Erskine. Burns attended. The minute of that meeting narrates that 'John Cathcart, Esq., John Hepburn, Esq., Mr Burn, and Mr Jones, were entered apprentices, and Mr Jones and Lord Torphichen were passed as fellowcraft and raised, and that the Earl of Errol, the Hon. William Gordon, (afterwards Earl of Kenmure), John Newal of Earlston, Captain Gillespie, and W. Campbell of Fairfield, were initiated. Farther, that the lodge was *visited by the Grand Lodge* – the Edinburgh Lodge – Mary's Chapel – Canongate and Leith – Leith and Canongate – Journeymen Masons' – St Luke's – Ruglen Royal Arch – and the Royal

Arch Lodge, Edinburgh.' Mr Dalrymple likewise introduced Burns to Erskine's brother-in-law, the Earl of Glencairn. On the same night Burns wrote his first Edinburgh letter to his friend, Mr Hamilton the writer – 'My Lord Glencairn and the Dean of Faculty, Mr H. Erskine, have taken me under their wing; and by all probability I shall soon be the tenth worthy and the eighth wise man of the world. . . . I have met in Mr Dalrymple of Orangefield what Solomon emphatically calls "a friend that sticketh closer than a BROTHER".' On Saturday, the 9th December, appeared the *Lounger's* Notice of the Kilmarnock Edition, and on the 13th, a Complimentary Epistle was published in the Edinburgh Evening Courant, in which Burns was acknowledged as 'The prince o' poets and o' ploughmen.'

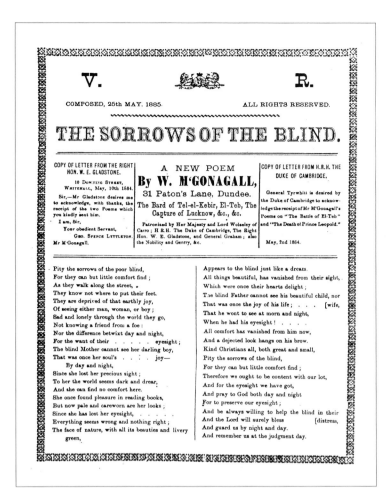

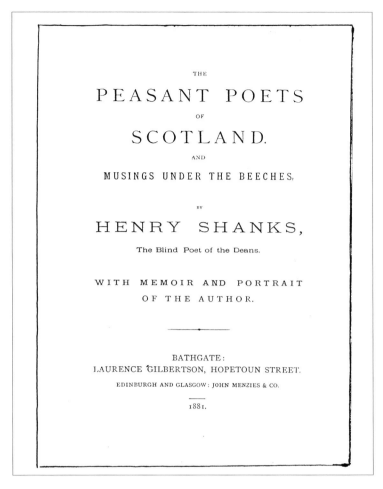

Wilson, the publisher of the Kilmarnock Edition, was astonished to find that on its publication it was all instantly sold off, and the demand continuing; yet (according to Gilbert Burns' letter to Dr Currie) he declined making a farther venture by undertaking a new edition. The poet explained this among his masonic friends in Edinburgh. 'Wilson,' he said, 'being a rigid Cameronian, had been averse even to undertaking the first edition, and when a second was proposed, he replied – "Ah, Rab, it winna do, unless ye begin your buik wi' mair sprinklin's o' serious bits".'

On the 13th Burns wrote Mr Ballantyne that 'my avowed patrons and patronesses are the Duchess of Gordon, the Countess of Glencairn, with my Lord and Lady Betty, the Dean of Faculty Sir John Whiteford. I have likewise warm friends among the literati, Professors Stewart, Blair, and Mr Mackenzie the "Man of Feeling." An unknown hand left me ten guineas. I have since discovered my generous unknown friend to be Patrick Miller, Esq., brother to the Justice-Clerk. Dugald Stewart and some of my learned friends put me in the periodical called the *Lounger*.'

The Canongate Kilwinning Lodge is situated in St John Street.

James W. Marshall *A Winter with Robert Burns* (1846)

THE PEASANT POETS

Robert Burns was an inspiration to all of Scotland's budding poets. The Scots had always been a literate nation and one hundred years ago there was a proliferation of interest in writing poetry and having it published in the newspapers and journals of the day. Those who could afford it enshrined their inspired verses in privately printed editions.

The Victorians blew out of all proportion Robert Burns's own tongue-in-cheek assertion that he was an 'untutored ploughman', and there was an increased interest in Scotland's supposed 'peasant poets' from James Hogg to John Hislop. Another such was Henry Shanks (1829–1900), 'The Blind Poet of the Deans, Bathgate'. He published his tribute to Burns *et al.* in 1881 and appended a collection of his own poems. One which received much adulation was 'The Curling Song', which Shanks wrote in Burnsian style:

Old England may her cricket boast,
Her wickets, bats, and a' that;
And proudly her Eleven toast,
Wi' right good will and a' that.
For a' that, and a' that,
It's but bairns' play for a' that;

Andrew Murray curling with Lord Strathallan, Strathallan Castle, Machaney Water, near Auchterarder,
Perthshire, 1864.

The channel stane on icy plain
Is king o' games for a' that.

And Erin's sons at wake and fair,
Wi' roar and yell and a' that,
May toss shillelahs in the air,
And crack their croons, and a' that;
For a' that, and a' that,
And better far than a' that,
Our roaring game aye keeps the flame
O' frien'ship bright for a' that.

When biting Boreas, keen and snell,
Wi' icy breath, and a' that,
Lays on the lochs his magic spell,
And stills the streams, and a' that;
For a' that, and a' that,
Cauld winter's snaw, and a' that,
Around the tee, wi' mirth and glee,
The curlers meet, for a' that.

But see yon cowerin' *cauldrife coof*,   [cold fool]
Wi' chitterin' teeth, and a' that,
In muffler, coat, and glove on 's loof
Wi' drap at 's nose for a' that;

For a' that, and 'a that,
As warm's a pie, and a' that,
The hardy Scot will cast his coat,
And play his game for a' that.

As in the serious game o' life,
Mischances aft befa' that,
So we must guard in curling strife
The winning stane, and a' that;
For a' that, and a' that,
Up through the port for a' that,
Some cunning hand, to skip's command,
May *wick* her out for a' that.   [cannon]

When bluid-red sets the winter sun,
Three ringing cheers, and a' that,
Proclaim the *bonspiel play* is won   [curling match]
By dint o' skill, and a' that;
For a' that, and a' that,
Wi' better luck, and a' that,
Opponents may, some ither day.

Now to the '*howff*' the curlers throng   [tavern]
For beef and greens, and a' that,
And spend the night wi' toast and song,

Henry Stanks, the 'Blind Poet of the Deans', Bathgate.

Aberdeen photographer Johnston Shearer's carte-de-visite *portrait, 1870, of the popular Aberdeen entertainer Charles 'McGonagall' Garvice. He entertained at parties reciting the execrable poetry of William McGonagall.*

Tho' Templars gibe at a' that;
For a' that, and a' that,
We'll pledge the toast for a' that,
Auld Scotland's name, and Scotland's fame,
And Scotland's game, for a' that.

And when the score o' life is made,
As made 'twill be, for a' that,
When *hin-han death's* last shot is played,   [last player]
And time's a hog, and a' that;
For a' that, and a' that,
Our besom friends for a' that,
We'll joyful meet, each rink complete,
Round higher tee for a' that.

The Scotsman, 27 December 1872

WILLIAM MCGONAGALL: 'POET AND TRAGEDIAN'

In Victorian days when most families made their own entertainment, either at the piano, on the violin or by recitation, the works of Scots poet William McGonagall (1825–1902) were especially popular because of their awfulness. The son of an Irish-born cotton weaver, the young McGonagall began his working life as a handloom weaver but also did some acting at Dundee's Royal Theatre. His first collection of poems was published in 1878. Thereafter he travelled widely in central Scotland giving recitations of his work which he sold as broadsheets. His *Poetic Gems* was published in 1890.

Chapter 6

GLIMPSES OF CHILDHOOD

O*n a number of social levels the First World War led to the emancipation of children. With fathers away at the Front, children enjoyed much greater personal liberty and a widening of work opportunities. During the war the legal restrictions on the hours children could work were largely overlooked, and the number of working children aged fourteen and under quadrupled.*

A hundred years ago gender identity was still rigid. Boys were taught that the main focus in their lives was public and that of girls private – men in the workforce and in sport, women at home. Males were thought of as more intelligent, girls as instinctive; men were strong, rough and biologically lustful, women were weak, delicate and lacking in desire. In all the social classes such divisions were deemed natural, thus boys were given mechanical practical toys, while girls were given dolls to nurse. Nevertheless, the well-to-do boy had a confusing experience. Up to the age of about nine, he lived entirely with women, his mother and his nanny. Fathers very rarely entered the nursery. Then the boys of wealthy families would be shunted off to boarding school, generally a wholly masculine environment.

At this time Scots children were, in general, better educated than ever before. The Education (Scotland) Act of 1872 had provided every parish and burgh in Scotland with an Elected School Board for the direction of education of children 'who might otherwise have grown up in ignorance and vice', as one contemporary commentator said. Up to 1890 parents were charged 3d per week for education, but thereafter it was virtually 'free'. Yet by the 1880s there were still 'half-time' schools for working-class children, who spent half their days at school and worked the rest in mills and other industries.

The children of poor folk were kept at home. There was little privacy in a labourer's cottage, still less in the city slums which consisted of an innumerable network of courts and closes (entries). The working population were constrained to live in one or the other.

For the upper and, to a lesser extent, middle classes, children were seldom an inconvenience. Their children were usually segregated from the adults, and they met only at short and programmed periods each day. Scrubbed, dressed up and on their best behaviour, upper-class children were allowed down from the nursery or schoolroom to be shown off to visitors, or to converse briefly with their parents. The Sunday walk (favoured by all classes), was a further opportunity for children to be in adult company.

For the working-class child, the principal diet consisted of bread and potatoes, while the rural child might enjoy eggs, milk and fruit in addition. Country children too, had the advantage of access to fields of produce – filched on the way to and from school – while the child of the well-to-do had a nursery diet of better nutritional value. Thus it was the dream of working-class mothers that their daughters 'go into service'; they believed they would enjoy a healthier life as domestic servants, although many fell into a life of poorly paid drudgery.

TERROR AT THE STUDIO

When I was a child the prospect of being photographed was very much on a par with that of the extraction of a tooth, only one was without the standing of a heroine or the payment of the 2s 6d damages. Unnaturally dressed and unusually brushed, I was taken into a strange Inquisition-like room. There an odiously familiar man perched me on some peculiarly uncomfortable piece of furniture and then petrified me with the startling prediction that 'Pussy' was about to emerge from the camera.

How vividly I remember the agonized suspense of awaiting her dreaded spring from the mysterious box. As a crowning horror to strained nerves the photographer then covered himself with a black pall, from the grim folds of which his voice emerged in the ghastly attempt at a playful 'Cuckoo!' Can one wonder at the glare of horror so faithfully reported by the camera, the staring eyes, the opened mouth?

Mothers who hope for good results must make sure the photographer they choose has relinquished such antiquated methods, and in place of these shock-tactics he must not have adopted the more modern tricks, such as ordering the sitter to say 'Good morning, good morning, good morning,' in order to make his mouth a certain shape.

So far from the studio being a Chamber of Horrors, to very young children a visit to it should seem a treat, not an ordeal. Instead of being frightened they must be amused. It is not sufficient that a child's head is no longer actually fixed; he must be given free play in every way, and allowed to roam about until, of his own accord, he temporarily settles and

Children from Chirnside, Berwickshire, make their way for a picnic at Coldingham Beach, on Empire Day. Empire Day had been inaugurated in 1902 in memory of Queen Victoria on 24 May, her birthday.

Scotland's Victorian studio photographs and street scenes show that in dress children were still treated as miniature adults. By the 1880s, though, the outfits of children from better-off homes were beginning to show some individuality more appropriate to childhood.

gives a chance to the photographer, who will have had the sense to equip a part of his studio like the nursery of one's dreams.

The camera should be camouflaged, and the room full of enchanting incident calculated to lure any child out of the disfiguring mask of self-consciousness. Instead of being made to blink by having one moth-eaten toy animal flourished before its eyes, the child – like a bee in a herbaceous border – should stray about at will until some imperative attraction rivets his attention, evoking that expression of rapt concentration which is one of the chief beauties of childhood.

Lady Cynthia Asquith, *The Child at Home* (1923)

TRIAL BY SAGO PUDDING

At tea I was always compelled to eat two formidable hunks of dry bread before I was allowed so much as to contemplate the blandishments of jam and cake. Now I see children going straight to the point. Unchidden, they at once stretch out their hands for the most rococo cake. They even paint the lily by spreading butter and jam on the same slice of bread. I well remember the first time my astonished eyes saw a 'grown-up' indulging in this particular form of excess, and how I expected that prompt divine retribution would make him choke.

One result of this prevailing leniency is that the emancipated children of today seldom either bolt or gorge. In one's eagerness to reach the more attractive stage of the meal, how

Children of the Royal School of Dunkeld, Culloden House, play in the shallows of the River Tay, Dunkeld, Perthshire, in 1891. In the background is the bridge built by Scots civil engineer Thomas Telford (1757–1834) in 1809.

one used to wolf the bread which blocked the way to the coveted cake, great boulders of unbitten food being washed down in gulps of milk. Nowadays, when I go to a children's party, I am amazed at the discretion and moderation displayed. Conscious that they may eat what they like when they like, they take their time and seem, for the most part, to know when they have had enough: in fact, I fear the 'weight of too much liberty' deprives them of some of the finest raptures of greed.

In my childhood there were no amiable ideas as to things you didn't like disagreeing with you. Far from thinking the gastric juices required propitiating, the theory was that the unpleasant was wholesome, or at any rate that the wholesome could not possibly be attractive. The fact that appreciated food is easier to digest is now scientifically proved.

It is no exaggeration to say that the whole of my babyhood was troubled by the dread of milk puddings. There is no greater physical torture than to be compelled to swallow anything strangely distasteful, and the horror is cumulative. The prospect of certain puddings became an absolute nightmare. I would rather have been whipped than confronted with a pile of glutinous adhesive sago. The awful sentence that anything left of your helping should resurrect cold for breakfast was grimly carried out, and I used to be interned whole afternoons with platefuls at which my very gorge rose.

Lady Cynthia Asquith

CHILDRENS' RHYMING GAMES

THE JOLLY MILLER. In this the players take partners – all except the miller, who takes his stand in the middle, while his companions walk round him in couples, singing:

> There was a jolly miller, who lived by himself,
> As the wheel went round he made his wealth;
> One hand in the hopper, and the other in the bag,
> As the wheel went round he made his grab.

At the word 'grab', every one must change partners. The miller then has the opportunity of seizing one: and if he succeeds in so doing, the one necessarily left alone must take his place, and so on.

QUEEN MARY. In this game the rhyme goes:

> Queen Mary, Queen Mary, my age is sixteen,
> My father's a farmer on yonder green,
> With plenty of money to dress me fu' braw,
> But nae bonnie laddie will tak' me awa'.
> One morning I rose, and I looked in the glass,
> Says I to myself I'm a handsome young lass;
> My hands by my side and I gave a ha! ha!
> Yet there's nae bonnie laddie will tak' me awa'.

It is played by girls only, who stand in a row, with one in front alone to begin with, who sings the verses, and chooses another from the line. The two then join hands and advance and retire, repeating together the verses, with suitable action, as the one had done before alone. At the close they select a third from the line; and the game proceeds thus until all are taken over.

WHUPPITY SCOORIE, though a game peculiar to Lanark, and to the boys of Lanark, and played only once a year, is yet worth mentioning. Its origin, like so many of the Lanark celebrations, is lost in the mists of antiquity, nevertheless it is still regularly played, and creates a sensation on its annual recurrence, affecting the old scarcely less than the young in the community. From the month of October till the month of February, inclusive, the bells in the Parish Church steeple there cease to ring at six o'clock in the evening, but resume on the first day of March. At the first peal of the bell then the children start and march three times round the church, after which a rush is made for the Wellgate Head, where they engage in a stand-up fight with the youth of New Lanark (who come that length to meet them), the weapons used being their bonnets attached to a long string. The fight over, the victors (generally the boys of the Old Town) return, marching in order, headed by one carrying a huge stick in exalted attitude, with a flag or handkerchief attached to it; and thus arranged, they parade the principal streets, singing, as their fathers and grandfathers sang before them:

Hooray, boys, hooray,
For we have won the day;
We've met the bold New Lanark boys,
And chased them doun the brae!

OATS AND BEANS AND BARLEY, a simple but pretty game, is played all over England, as well as in most parts of Scotland, with varying rhymes. In Perthshire the lines run:

Oats and beans and barley grows,
Oats and beans and barley grows;
But you nor I nor nobody knows
How oats and beans and barley grows.
First the farmer sows his seeds,
Then he stands and takes his ease;
Stamps his feet, and claps his hands,
Then turns around to view his lands.
Waiting for a partner,
Waiting for a partner;
Open the ring and take one in,
And kiss her in the centre.

The players form a ring by joining hands. One child – usually a boy – stands in the middle. The ring moving round, sing the first four lines. These completed, the ring stands, and still singing, each player gives suitable action to the succeeding words; showing how the 'farmer sows his seeds', and how he 'stands and takes his ease', etc. At the tenth line all wheel round. They then rejoin hands, still singing, and at the words,

Children gather in Easter Street, Duns, Berwickshire, at the junction with Middlemiss's Temperance Hotel, Currie Street. Several of the Victorian temperance groups, like the Good Templars, sponsored children's outings.

'Open the ring and take one in', the child in the middle chooses from the ring a partner (a girl, of course), whom he leads to the centre and kisses as requested. The two stand together, while the ring, moving again, sing the marriage formula:

> Now you've married, you must obey,
> Must be true to all you say;
> You must be kind, you must be good,
> And help your wife to chop the wood.

Robert Ford, *Childrens' Rhymes* (1908)

TRADITIONAL STREET SONGS AND VERSES FOR CHILDREN

A Counting-out Rhyme

> One two three four
> Mary at the cottage door:
> Five six seven eight
> Eating cherries off a plate.

A Skipping Rhyme

> Mrs Brown went to town
> Riding on a pony:
> When she came back
> She lost her hat
> And called on Miss Maloney.

Three Skipping Chants

> House to let –
> Apply within:
> As I go out
> My neighbour comes in.

> House to let –
> Apply within:
> A woman put out
> For drinking gin.

> House to let –
> Apply within:
> A woman put out
> For showing her thing.

The 42nd [Black Watch Regiment]

> Wha saw the Forty-second
> Wha saw them gang awa'
> Wha saw the Forty-Second
> Mairchin' thro' the Broomielaw?

> Some o' them had *buits* and stockin's   [boots]
> Some o' them had *nane* at a'   [none]

Some o' them had kilts and sporrans
Mairchin' thro' the Broomielaw.

Counting-out Rhyme

> Eetle ottle black bottle
> Eetle ottle out:
> Shining on the mantelpiece
> Like a silver threepenny-piece. . . .

A Skipping Song

> One o'clock the gun went off
> I dare not stay no longer
> If I do mother will say
> Playing with the boys up yonder.

> Stockings red, garters blue,
> Trimmed all round with silver:
> A red red rose upon my head
> And a gold ring on my finger.

> Heigh-ho, my Johnnie-O,
> My bonny bonny Johnnie-O:
> The only one that I love best
> Is my bonny bonny Johnnie-O.

'Victoria' or 'Bonfire' Day:

> The Twenty-fourth of May
> Is the Queen's Birthday:
> If we dinnie get a holiday
> We'll *a'* run away!   [all]

Buffalo Bill

> Buffalo Bill
> He shoots to kill
> Never missed
> And he never will.

My Love's a Soldier

> My love's a soldier
> In lands far away:
> A true-he'rted laddie
> Sae gallant and gay.

> His ways they are so winning
> And I shall wait a while
> On my bonny laddie
> O' the rank and file!

> A day seems a month
> And a month seems a year:
> But my bonny laddie
> He'll soon be here.

Auntie Mary

Auntie Mary
Had a canary
Up the leg o' her drawers:
It whistled for hours
And frichted the Boers
And won the Victoria Cross!

I Widnie be a Bobbie

I *widnie* be a Bobbie   [would not]
A big fat Bobbie
To wash my mother's lobby
Wi' washin' *sodie*.   [soda]

And when the sodie meltit
I got my ear *skelpit*   [smacked]
And tho' I couldnie help it
By God I felt it!

At the Cross

At the Cross, at the Cross,
Where we played at pitch-and-toss
And the Bobbie come
And chased us a' away:

We ran and we ran
Till we fell owre a man
And that was the end
Of the play.

FIRST TROUSERS

Little boys in those days did not wear trousers until they were about four years old. Now-a-days both boys and girls wear a sort of caricature of trousers by the time they are six months old, but even up to the beginning of the present century boys were dressed somewhat like little girls until they reached the age of three or four, and I can remember when I was a little girl at school in the country being chased round the playground by a boy in petticoats who was six or seven years old! This little chap, as I say, had got his first suit – trousers, vest and little coat or jacket – while his mother was ill, and the first morning he was dressed in his new rig-out he marched into the dining-room where his father was talking to the doctor, and hands in pockets, head and shoulders thrown back, exclaimed – 'There's three men in our house to-day.' Little boys in those days and especially at an earlier date were always in a state of exultation on that first day that they ceased to be a girl.

Margaret Ross

Scout group on Coldingham Sands, c. 1910. The Boy Scout movement was founded by the First Chief Scout Sir Robert Baden-Powell (1857–1941) and began in 1908; a parallel organisation for girls, the Girl Guides, was founded by Baden-Powell in 1910.

Children on holiday at Earlston, in the Lauderdale Valley, Berwickshire. In this picture of the early 1900s outside C.L. McDonald's General Drapery Establishment, two girls sport bicycles, much prized possessions in low-wage communities of the period.

TOUGHENING UP

My earliest recollection is . . . of the isle of Arran. It is of being chased, in the arms of my nurse, by a bull; and I have even now a vivid remembrance of a white gate reached for safety by a panting woman. My next clear recollection is more pathetic: the sands of St Andrews and my nurse after the manner of her tribe, at least in those days, ducking me mercilessly in the sea. Choking and breathless I could stand this tyranny no longer. With a wild 'will to freedom' I tore myself from her grasp and naked as I was ran for dear liberty along the sands. . . .

Cosmo Gordon Lang (1868)

FILM STAR MARCHING CHANT

The moon shines bright on Charlie Chaplin
His boots are cracklin'
For the want o' black'nin'
And his baggy little trousers needin' mendin'
Before they send him
To the Dardanelles!

THE DAYS BEFORE 1914

In the 1900s Edinburgh looked more like a country town. Children could walk without danger to a drinking-fountain placed at the centre of the traffic in the West End, and on that island could leisurely sample the ice-cold water from one of the iron cups that were chained there.

Apart from cable-cars, most of the vehicles were drawn by horses. Riding on the back axle of a horse-cab became a favourite pastime when the opportunity occurred. Passers-by would call out 'Cull callant, [boy] ahint [behind]!' and the cabbie would flick his whip backwards to dislodge the free traveller. Some girls enjoyed this recreation almost as much as boys. Most children considered the waters of a horse's trough perfectly admirable for sailing paper boats in. And at every tram-terminus, especially during the months of May and June, a glorious, almost luxuriant, countryside would burst into being, with hedges smothered in flourish or wild roses.

James T.R. Ritchie

CHILDREN IN PUBLIC

Children in my early days were looked upon partly as a nuisance and partly as a kind of animate toy, to be shown, if they were sufficiently attractive, to callers. We were always brought down and shown after lunch, but were never expected to utter, and were consequently all abominably shy. The first time I began to feel a little more sure of myself was when something I had said to our nurse was repeated by the nursemaid to my mother's maid. The nurse, who was an inveterate talker, had turned to me and said, 'Silence is golden,' when I had attempted to make a remark; and I had

Workmen and apprentices at the coachbuilders of Goble and Loutit, Birnam, Perthshire, 1866. Even in rural areas there was a pool of potential apprentices in the harsh economic climate of mid-Victorian Scotland.

responded, 'Talking is lead.' The punishment which she promptly inflicted on me was quite outweighed by the unexpected applause I got from the visitors after lunch that day, when my mother told the story. It made me feel that I was not quite the little fool that Nanna Haig would have me think I was. As a rule, however, the maxim that 'children should be seen and not heard' was thrust down our throats until we were well into our teens.

It was an unheard-of thing for children up to the age of fourteen to be allowed to eat the same food as grown-ups. The only meal we had in the dining-room was luncheon, when special but entirely unappetising food was provided for us; and I remember my own feelings – shared, I am sure, by my sisters – at seeing and smelling the delicious-looking dishes offered to the more mature humans. I confess to have appreciated good food all my life, and, looking back, can quite understand why I dissolved into tears when my governess informed me that food was totally unnecessary in Heaven.

Even at children's parties one seldom heard an animated prattle, except among the grown-ups. I remember being hauled out of bed one evening to be taken to a fancy-dress ball at old Lady Conyngham's house.

My sisters had dresses covered with daisies, which they had worn, as bridesmaids, at the wedding of a cousin; these were considered sufficiently fancy, and they were told to say 'Spring' when asked what they represented. Presumably for economy's sake, no fancy dress had been bought for me, and I was therefore put to bed on the night of the party instead of being taken to it. We had often met Lady Conyngham's daughters in the Square, and they were always very kind to

us, especially Lady Jane, then a beautiful girl of about fifteen. When my mother arrived at the house with my two sisters, she was at once asked by her hostess's daughters, 'Where's George?' The result was that the carriage was sent back, and I was hauled out of bed and dressed in the sailor suit which all small boys of that period were accustomed to wear all day and every day. To this moment I remember boys at that party asking me, with an undisguised sneer, what I was supposed to represent, and a small voice answering: 'A Jack Tar.'

George Cornwallis-West

CHILDREN IN THE MINES

I have a belt round my waist and a chain passing between my legs, and I go on my hands and feet. The road is very steep, and we have to hold by a rope, and when there is no rope, by anything we can catch hold of. There are six women and about six boys in the pit I work in: it is very hard work for a woman. The pit is very wet where I work, and the water comes over our clogs always, and I have seen it up to my thighs: it rains in at the roof terribly; my clothes are wet through almost all day long. I never was ill in my life but when I was lying-in. My cousin looks after my children in the daytime. I am very tired when I get home at night; I fall asleep sometimes before I get washed. I am not so strong as I was, and cannot stand my work so well as I used to do. I have drawn until I have had the skin off me; the belt and chain is worse when we are in the family way. My feller has beaten me many a time for not being ready. I were not used to it at first, and he had little patience. I have known many a man beat his drawer.

Oral memory, Betty Harris, 1850s

AN OFFICE BOY'S LAMENT

THEY made me vacate in the spring,
    When weather was cold, raw, and bleak;
Still present was winter's chill sting,
    As I shivered in Largs a long week.

Now I am here in the city –
    'Summer' holidays o'er for a year –
And as I pen this sad ditty,
    I silently shed a salt tear.

For in town the heat is torrid,
    In the office I swelter and stew,
Everything's hateful and horrid,
    I long for the sea, calm and blue.

Around me all talk is of coast –
    Others' holidays quickly draw near –

And while I remain at my post
    They will bask in a boat 'neath a pier.

Or laze on a heathery hill,
    By zephyrs fragrant, lightly fanned,
Or harken to a purling rill,
    Or slowly stroll on wave beat sand.

'Mong breezes soft and balmy cool,
    The governor golfs the day long,
Far, far from ink pots and high stool,
    In earshot of birds' happy song.

The cashier has gone to Dunoon,
    In mo'car Brown's 'way on a tour,
The 'junior' sports gay ties at Troon,
    The 'Twelfth' will see Jones on a moor.

So weary and parched I am here,
    Musing deeply of waves' mystic wash;
I'll hie me to hostelry near
    And drown care with a straw and a squash.

The Bailie, 1903

Middle class girls of Kelvingrove, Glasgow, with their teachers, c. 1880. Much school learning of the day was drearily factual in content and repetitive in method.

CHILDHOOD RESTRICTIONS

Children at that time were kept in great order, and generally forbidden to do anything they particularly liked – more, I think, on general principle than for any sufficient reason. Their books were then of a totally different sort from those of today; most of them contained poetry, or rather versification, inculcating good behaviour, especially with regard to that moderation which childhood usually, and perhaps not unnaturally, abominates. The highly salutary precepts enjoined in books such as Mrs Turner's *Cautionary Stories*, were in great favour with parents. Some of the lines in this volume with regard to gluttony are highly characteristic of infantile education as it was understood in the past –

>   Mamma, why mayn't I, when I dine,
>   Eat ham and goose, and drink port wine?
>   And why mayn't I, as well as you,
>   Eat pudding, soup, and mutton, too?

Then comes the quiet dignity of the reply –

>   Because, my dear, it is not right,
>   To spoil the youthful appetite.

The daily life of a child seventy years ago or so was of a far simpler description than at present, when even quite small children are in something of touch with public events. Unlike the young people of today, who regard their elders with good-humoured toleration, if not with a feeling of positive superiority, we stood in awe of our older relatives; as for our parents, their wishes were regarded more or less as irrevocable decrees.

My father was an autocrat, whose rule over his family was absolutely unquestioned. Well do I remember how, at breakfast (which all of us were always expected to attend), my mother would on certain days catch my eye and significantly look down at her plate where her knife and fork had been carefully crossed – a sign to the family that its head was in no mood for conversation. My father, though a most good-natured man, was at times easily roused to temporary fury by anything which clashed with his mood.

Lady Dorothy Nevill, *Under Five Reigns* (1910)

CLASSROOM WISDOM

It has often been told, but is worth repeating, how a pupil teacher was doing his level best to make the children remember Samson's mighty deeds with the jawbone of an ass, and, recapitulating, he asked, 'What did Samson slay ten thousand Philistines with? Eh?' No reply came. Then, pointing to his jawbone, he asked, 'What is this?' And at once the answer belched proudly from half-a-dozen throats in unison, 'The jawbone of an ass!'

'Why is it,' asked a teacher, 'the sun never sets on the British possessions?' 'Because,' slowly responded an ingenuous youngster, 'the British possessions are in the north, south, and east, and the sun always sets in the west.'

During a recent School Board examination in the west of Scotland, the examiner asked a little girl to explain what was meant by the expression, *He was amply rewarded*. 'Paid for't,' was her instant reply. 'No, no; you are wrong. Suppose you have to go into a baker's shop and buy a half-quarter loaf, and lay down fourpence, would you say you had amply rewarded the baker?' Unhesitatingly she replied 'Yes.' 'Why?' 'Because the loaf's only twopence-three-farthings,' was the unlooked-for answer.

Robert Ford

THE SCHOOLBOY'S LAY

>   THE school is over once again,
>   We'll shout hip, hip, hooray;
>   Let none despond, for now has dawned
>   The demonstration day.
>
>   We'll gather in the old, old place,
>   A merry, happy crew,
>   To show to all, who throng the hall,
>   What we've been taught to do.
>
>   We'll sing the dear familiar songs,
>   Songs learned in the school,
>   'Hail, Jocund June', 'The Mirthful Moon',
>   And 'On an Evening Cool'.
>
>   The audience loudly will applaud
>   When we resume our seats,
>   And then prepare to list to Clare
>   Recite 'The *Poke* of Sweets'.   [bag]
>
>   They'll hear, with slowly rising hair,
>   The 'Ghost of Trumpy Grim',
>   Mayhap the lay of 'Lucy Gray',
>   Or 'Death of Little Jim'.
>
>   At length the great event draws near,
>   And high all spirits rise,
>   While quite jocose are all of those
>   Whose children won a prize.
>
>   The gent. who occupies the chair,
>   In speech that's quite a treat,
>   To all accords, who've gained rewards,
>   Congratulations neat.
>
>   But to the boys who got no prize
>   He says, 'midst much applause,
>   My friends, don't fret, you'll sparkle yet,
>   All great men got the *tawse*.   [strap]

Prime Minister William Ewart Gladstone (1809–98) glances at his speech before laying the foundation stone of a boys' boarding house at Glenalmond College, Perth, 1 October 1891.

So when we've made our bashful bow,
  And clutch with joy our prize,
We gaily sing 'God Save the King',
  Pride of our parents' eyes.

The Bailie, 1902

PREPARATORY SCHOOL DAYS

BOYS between the ages of eight and twelve are often nasty little creatures. Their minds are not sufficiently developed to have any sense of justice; with them it is purely a question of the survival of the fittest, and the supervision of older boys or masters is essential if the weaker element is to be saved from leading a life of hellish torment.

I was sent, after leaving Grammar School, to a preparatory school – I refrain from mentioning which, but there are three schools there; suffice it to say that it contained so many sprigs of aristocracy that it went by the name of 'the House of Lordlings'. I have often discussed the past with men of my own age who were at that school, and we have all agreed that we would not go back there for a million pounds. Hardly one of the masters was a gentleman. We were taught well,

I admit, but if it had not been for the fact that our parents sent us hampers of food which we were supposed to share with the other boys seated at the same table, we should scarcely have been fed at all. As it was, if one happened to be unpopular with the boy whose hamper was being shared, one got nothing at breakfast or tea but bread and butter. The only meal actually provided by the school was the mid-day meal, with its everlasting stringy beef or mutton, both invariably over-roasted.

George Cornwallis-West

SCHOOL BULLIES

Bullying at that school had developed into a fine art. I was a very delicate child, in fact an overgrown slab of misery, unable to take part to any great extent in games; I was in consequence made to suffer. One of the chief amusements of the bullies in our bedroom was to tie scarves to each wrist and ankle, stretch the unfortunate victim on the bed and pretending that he was 'on the rack', only there wasn't much pretence about it. Another form of amusement was to make small boys eat flies.

Fettes College, East Fettes Avenue, Edinburgh. Merchant and underwriter Sir William Fettes (1750–1836) left £166,000 for the establishment of a school. Here the newly built college (by David Bryce, 1864–70) is seen with the builder's shed still in use.

Gymnasium of Fettes College (built 1878). The first boys arrived in October 1870, and girls one hundred years later. The gym became the east concert hall. Fettes was the first purpose-built boarding school in Scotland.

The whole school at Fettes College, c. 1880. Dr A.W. Potts, headmaster, stands centre back (in cap and gown); he was headmaster from 1870 until his death in November 1889.

The headmaster himself was, I honestly believe, a sadist; I am certain it afforded him intense pleasure to administer the severest thrashings, having first deprived the boy of any form of protection. He once, while I was there, thrashed a boy until he fainted.

Unfortunately for the bullies, I completely upset their apple-cart by attempting to commit suicide, not entirely on my own initiative, as it was suggested by one of my aggressors, who said, 'Let's make young West drink ink.' Before I could be prevented I had swallowed most of the contents of one of the desk inkpots. Then they really were frightened. A master came in, realised that something was amiss, saw my mouth covered with ink and was told what had happened. I was promptly given an emetic. A court of inquiry was then held and, greatly to my delight, three of the worst offenders received probably as good a thrashing as they ever had in their lives. To their credit be it said that the rest of the boys in the school realised that things had gone too far, and the known bullies were put in Coventry for the rest of the half.

At the end of my last term at a private school I developed quinsy and was a week late in returning from the holidays. Matters were not improved by an operation for tonsils, done by the local doctor (my grandmother had died in 1887 and my father had inherited from her Newlands Manor, which he used as a summer residence) in an arm-chair in the study, without an anaesthetic. I bled so much that in the middle of the operation the doctor himself became what we should now call 'hot and bothered', so much so that he left the other tonsil as it was, with subsequent disastrous results. However, by the time I went to Eton, at the Christmas half of 1888, I was quite all right, and looked forward with joy to the new life.

I had not been at public school more than a day or two before I began to appreciate the comparative freedom which can be enjoyed there. After my private school, I felt as a prisoner must feel who has been released from a term of imprisonment, except that imprisonment, even in those days, did not carry with it the tortures which were inflicted on me and many others.

Boys, when they become members of a public school, appear to undergo a complete metamorphosis. They seem to shed that skin which makes them unjust, thoughtless and cruel; and gradually to assume a more generous attitude towards their fellows. They have an example set them by the older boys, who are themselves arriving at manhood and learning to appreciate the more serious side of life.

I was fortunate in being sent to Walter Durnford's house at public school, one of the best there. My tutor was beloved by all. Scrupulously fair, he always studied the interests of the boys in his house and trusted them implicitly, with the result that it was a code of honour in the house that no one should ever let his tutor down. If anyone did, and was found out, he deservedly got a pretty bad time from the boys in the house.

George Cornwallis-West

VICTORIAN CHILDREN'S REPARTEE

'Did any of you ever see an elephant's skin?' asked the master of an infant school. 'I have,' shouted a six-year-old at the foot of the class. 'Where?' 'On the elephant.'

A little boy of my acquaintance, while yet a pupil in the infant department, was one day given a slate, more to engage his attention than aught else. But he had some notion of drawing, and when the teacher came round she was astonished to find he had set down a fair picture of a bird on a bough. 'Ha! who drew this?' she asked. 'Mysel',' was the canny Scotch reply. 'And who's mysel'?' she queried. 'Oh, I'm fine,' was the second response, not less Scotch than the first. The English reader, of course, won't fairly understand the word 'fine' as spoken there; but every Scotsman will, as also how 'who's' may be mistaken for 'how's.'

There is another 'fine' story. It was asked of a class, 'How did the Israelites get across the Red Sea?' 'Fine,' exclaimed a youth with brightening eyes; ''twas the 'Gyptians was droon'd.'

'What do you mean by a temperate region?' asked an inspector of a class, putting due emphasis on the word temperate. 'The region, sir,' responded a boy, 'where they drinks only temperants drinks.'

Not along ago a class of boys were being examined on the different kinds of wood; and one little chap was asked to name the specimen (a piece of mahogany) which was held in the examiner's hand. He hesitated, and the inspector, by way of suggestion, remarked, 'Why, don't you know the materials that your mother's drawers are made of?' This seemed to simplify the matter, and, amidst a roar of laughter, came the quick reply – 'Flannelette!'

'Name anything friable,' said a teacher. 'Ham,' was the ready answer.

'What is a papal bull?'

'A golden calf.'

'What is ice?'

'Water fast asleep.'

'What is a skeleton?'

'A man without any meat on it.'

A teacher was examining a class on the battle of Bannockburn, and asked, 'Who killed de Bohun?' No one knew. He raised his arm in an attitude of striking, and yelled, with flashing eyes, 'Who killed de Bohun, I say?' A little fellow near him, who expected the blow, raised his arm in a defensive attitude, and whined, 'Oh, please, sir, it wasna me.'

'What is meant by faith?' was one day asked of a class. 'Faith,' responded a thoughtful youth, 'is the faculty which enables us to believe things that we know to be not true.'

In the lesson of a class of country boys not long ago, the words 'above the average' occurred, and the lady teacher asked if any one could tell what the word 'average' meant. There was no response for a time, and she passed the question from one to another until a more than average specimen eagerly responded, 'It's a thing that hens lay on.' The teacher was dumbfounded, and asked for an explanation. 'Well,' drawled the budding Solomon, 'my mother says that our hens lay each four eggs a week – on an average.'

Quite like that is the story of a small boy into whose head a teacher was one day labouring almost in vain to get, as he thought, even the faintest correct notion of the first rules in arithmetic. 'Look here now, Johnnie,' he said at length, 'if I were to give you two rabbits and your father were to give you three rabbits, how many rabbits would you then have?' 'Six.' 'No, no'; and the teacher set out bits of chalk to show how he could only have five. 'Ah, but,' drawled out Johnnie, 'I have a rabbit at hame already.'

Robert Ford

AN ARCHBISHOP'S CHILDHOOD MEMORIES

The real scene of my childhood was the garden of the Bank House, Morningside. . . . I suppose it was quite a small garden, but it was my world, from the age of four to nine. It was my own world, where my imagination for once had its unclouded day. It was a world of 'make-believe'. Lessons there were, even for a while at an old dame's school: brothers there were, three of them. Sometimes I made the younger, next to me, the unwilling and mystified vassal to my dreams. But the world I remember is the garden – the trees behind which robber-knights were stalked and slain; the earth under a shrub where on a cold day unknown to all I sat, self-stripped, indulging in all the pathos of a beggar-child; the bundle of sticks on which I stood enduring the fancied flames as a Christian martyr; the great black roaring cat, who was to me the Devil walking about seeking whom he might devour – I can see him now, stealthy and sinister, creeping along the wall – at whom I threw every missile of fervent and pious wrath. In all that world I reigned supreme, fancy free. . . . These were the years, never to be repeated, when I was master of my own realm, the glorious realm of imagination, the 'land of make-believe'. . . . Of course there will be pains as well as pleasure in the kingdom of an imaginative child. How well I remember, during many nights after my mother had been reading the *Pilgrim's Progress*, watching in terror Apollyon's face on the wall, rolling his fiery tongue!

Or again, a little later, when I suppose I was eight or perhaps nine. It was at Ardrishaig on Loch Fyne and my young eyes saw the sun setting in the west. I became convinced that some great adventure or discovery was awaiting me there. I must at all costs go and find it. It was the call of the unknown, of the Ideal World. I set off, walked and ran for miles along the banks of the Crinan Canal, which led westwards. I became tired and hungry, and still the thrill I was seeking never came. Weary and disillusioned, I sank down on the bank. There the realities of life – the pursuers and the punishments – overtook me and I learned the bitter lesson of life, that ideals must ever be sought but never found.

Cosmo Gordon Lang

Chapter 7
VEHICLES VARIOUS

One hundred years ago Scotland's transportation was still dominated by horse-drawn vehicles. Every town and village had its own blacksmith and stabling facilities. Street dangers in those days included bolting horses, which might have in their wake a heavy dray cart spilling its goods until a courageous passer-by grabbed the flying reins and brought the animal to a standstill. Horse traffic ensured that public thoroughfares were noisy, and along private roads layers of straw would be placed outside the homes of the ill to deaden the clattering vibrations of iron-shod wheels and horses' hooves.

As the twentieth century evolved the new combustion-engined 'horseless carriage' began to dominate the streets and a whole new set of public highway legislation made its way on to the statute books. The great and the good of the period all inspired fashions in motoring, from the king to Scottish statesmen and Prime Minister A.J. Balfour (1848–1930). The motor car was not universally welcomed – a whole group of clergy, innkeepers and farmers regularly berated the 'dangerous contraptions' in pulpit and bar.

Black's Shilling Guide to Scotland (1906) warned of the dangers of certain Scottish roads, such as those between Tyndrum and Ballachulish, that might ruin tyres 'worth £20 apiece'. And the exposed passengers of open-topped cars were warned to look out for potentially decapitating low branches. Yet despite these well-meant warnings the motor vehicle replaced the horse and entered the history of Scottish travel.

IMPORTANT DATES

1848	Express trains introduced on London to Edinburgh route, via the West Coast; journey took twelve and a half hours.
1850	1 April: London to Aberdeen trains traverse East Coast route.
1865	'Red Flag Act' – wherein a guide was required to walk in front of a motor vehicle to show its coming. Speed restrictions for cars introduced: 4 mph (rural roads) 2 mph (town roads).
1871	Horse tramcars appear in Edinburgh.
1872	1d per mile fare introduced for 3rd Class Rail Travel.
1876	Through trains from Edinburgh to Glasgow introduced.
1877	26 September: first train crosses Tay Bridge.
1878	Cyclists' Touring Club formed.
1879	28 December: Tay Bridge disaster; death toll: 75.
1883	First North British Railway through trains to Aberdeen.
1887	13 June: New Tay Railway Bridge opened.
1888	Ayrshire-born J.B. Dunlop re-invents pneumatic tyres.
1890	Forth Railway Bridge opened.
1891	Cable tramcars introduced by Edinburgh Corporation.
1893	Caledonian Railway takes over Port Glasgow–Wemyss Bay route; the latter the key station for embarkation for steamers to Rothesay and the Isles.
1896	Act emancipates motoring; now allowed to reach 12 mph.

A dog-cart and its gentleman driver outside the Cross Keys Inn, Lilliesleaf, Roxburghshire, in the 1890s. The dog-cart was one of the most popular personal vehicles in Scotland's rural areas.

SCOTLAND'S TOP SIX POPULAR CARRIAGES, 1837–1901

Named after Henry Peter Brougham, 1st Baron Brougham and Vaux (1778–1868), the Scottish jurist and politician who imported one from Paris, this carriage developed as a single-horse closed carriage for town use. They cost £100–£180.

The sociable landau appeared around 1851 and developed as a two-horse open carriage to take advantage of the improved road surfaces pioneered by Scots engineer and metropolitan roads supervisor John Loudon McAdam (1756–1836). A two-horse version cost around £275.

A wagonette was first built, the records show, for Albert the Prince Consort, but its popularity boomed after the report of the Great Exhibition of 1862. It became the 'perfection of a family country carriage' at around £50.

The park phaeton was essentially a 'lady's carriage', constructed for use with ponies or horses. Used both in town and country from the 1870s, the carriage had a hood for inclement weather and an exposed seat at the rear for the footman. They were relatively expensive at £100.

The basket pony phaeton was drawn by a small pony or donkey and was meant for country use and for the transportation of children. Second-hand carriages of this type were available for as little as £5.

The dog-cart was the most popular of the two-wheeled carriages. They began as sporting carriages around the 1840s and were seen in Scottish country districts across the turn of the century. They cost between £25 and £60.

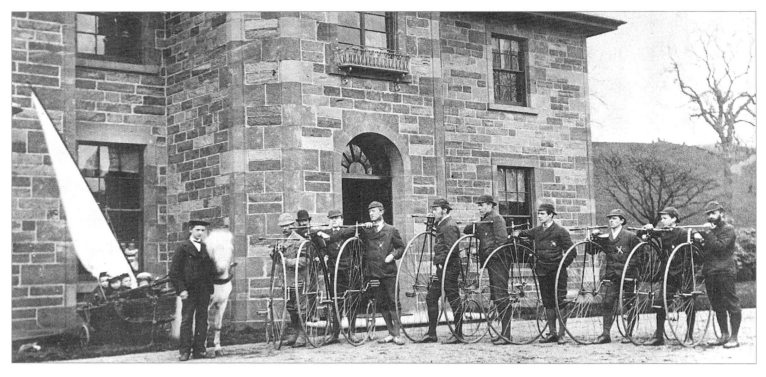

Edinburgh Cycle Club visits Comrie, Perthshire, c. 1875.

A 3½ hp Cheviot motorcycle made by F. Chappel of Berwick-upon-Tweed; it was first used as a 'one-off' bike at the First Scottish Six-Day Trials of 1909.

1897   *Royal Automobile Club founded.*
1900   *Electric tramcars introduced to Dundee.*
1903   *Compulsory licence plates appear for cars; speed limits raised to 20 mph.*
1905   *Formation of the Automobile Association.*
1907   *First motor taxi-cab registered at Edinburgh.*
1908   *First motor car produced specifically for doctors; built at Alexandria, Dumbartonshire.*
1910   *First electric tramcar commences at Edinburgh.*
1915   *Worst train disaster in UK; triple collision at Quintinshill, near Gretna Green, Dumfriesshire. Death toll: 227.*

ENTER THE BIKE

Dry weather produces the cyclist, the worst pest which infests country paths. With his shrill bell singing like an alarm clock, he scoots along the highway, swallowing acres of dust, which he judiciously irrigates with oceans of beer. At quaint village hostelries he clamours for ham and eggs in a way which would delight the heart of Sir Tom, and full of the flesh-pots of Egypt he hurtles o'er the earth – a Mercury on wheels. Sometimes he varies his flight by charging violently into the back of a man intent on studying nature, and the sound of his bell is always calculated to develop the leaping powers of the pedestrian, who springs agonisingly for sanctuary to the nearest pavement. As the poet hath it:

From off the road leaps Sunny Jim;
A cyclist's bell has startled him.

THE CYCLIST

THE untamed cyclist takes his final scorch along the roads on the September holiday before stowing away his machine in the gloomy depths of a cellar. For many weeks now the philosophic pedestrian may saunter along the country lane without the agonising dread of being a gory feature in a bicycle accident. The joyous youngster may gambol in the roadway without receiving the profane remarks of the flying wheelman. Honest-hearted carters do not need to worry lest a cyclist run into them. Cyclists have a habit of running into things – even if it only be a public-house, but winter's muddy roads and wet weather blights the pests.

The Bailie, 1903

THE TAY BRIDGE CATASTROPHE

ON Sunday evening, the 29th of December, 1879, the railway bridge that then spanned the Tay at Dundee for a large part of its length, was blown into the river. Encaged in the girders that gave way to the westerly gale, racing at 100 miles to the hour, was a train fairly well filled with passengers, all of whom were drowned.

As I had much to do with the bridge, I might recall some incidents regarding that appalling catastrophe. The bridge, of course, was too slim for its height and too narrow. The contractors were a firm of Germans, and as was proved in the inquiry, did a great deal of jerry work in a job that had been taken too cheap; but it must be confessed the design was too flimsy. The engineer, with the ominous name of Bouch, died shortly after the accident. Some said of a broken heart, and no wonder, if true.

To accommodate the people of Newport and Wormit, on the south side of the Tay, it was arranged that a supply of water should be given from the Dundee reservoirs. This supply was conveyed across the river by a nine-inch pipe placed at one side of the bridge, encased in a wooden box stuffed with sawdust. My firm contracted to supply the wooden casing and sawdust, and, foolishly, also guaranteed the due execution of the job by the joinery firm who had undertaken it. This firm became bankrupt just after the job was started, and I had to finish the box with my own people. This was very precarious work. It was only allowed to be done on Sundays, between trains, of which there were only two. It took several Sundays to take out, lay, and join up and fill the box, and it was just finished, and the first coat of paint put on, when the bridge fell.

No Dundee people still alive can ever forget the horror of the day that dawned after that dreadful accident. When the truth became known the whole city was stunned, and every one dumb with amazement at the dreadfulness of the event. It took the city many long years to cast off the gloom that fell upon it.

We lived at that time in Airlie Place, just opposite the bridge. The gale that had sprung up in the afternoon became intense about 7 o'clock; chimney cans and roof flashings began to be blown about, and I suggested to my wife that we should take a walk out and see the unusual sight. We got with

Construction began on a New Tay Railway Bridge in 1882, following the destruction of the 1871–7 bridge in the storm of 1879. Here, girders for the new bridge are placed in position, 3 March 1886.

difficulty, holding on to each other and walking at an acute angle, as far as the Magdalen Green. Trees, chimney cans, and palings were being scattered, and we were very glad to get home uninjured. The bridge could not be seen for the spindrift which blew down the river twenty or thirty feet high, but through it, as we passed along, we saw something like an avalanche of red cinders falling, and as we learned in the morning, that was the very moment the bridge fell.

I lost a faithful clerk, James Leslie, in the accident. His parents lived on the south side of the river, a mile or two off. He usually walked to Newport and took the ferry back, but on that wild night had taken the train. It was my melancholy duty to identify his body when it was recovered from the river. In one pocket he had a Bible, in the other a copy of Longfellow's poems that I had given him. So severe was the gale that fragments of the railway carriages were washed ashore at West Ferry Beach, more than four miles distant, within half an hour of the accident. All the bodies were recovered by means of grappling hooks about half a mile east of the scene of the accident.

Sir John Fleming

SPANNING THE FORTH

In 1873 the Forth Bridge Company was formed for the purpose of carrying out the design by Sir Thomas Bouch of a suspension bridge with two large spans of 1600 ft each. The capital was raised by the four principal railway companies interested in the East Coast traffic – namely, the Great Northern, the North-Eastern, the Midland, and the North-British, and the companies came to an understanding among themselves that they would between them send so much traffic across the bridge as would suffice to pay a dividend of 6 per cent per annum on the contract sum. The Act authorising the construction of the bridge was passed in the

Construction of the Forth Rail Bridge in progress 1883–1890.

same year, 1873, and a contract signed with Messrs W. Arrol and Co., of Glasgow.

The central towers from which the main chains are suspended were to have been 550 ft above high water, while the rail level would be at such height as to leave a clear headroom of 150 ft above high water between the piers. The central tower on Inchgarvie was over 500 ft long, which brought the foundations upon the sloping rock down to a depth of over 110 ft below high water. There were two lines of rails carried at a distance of 100 ft from each other, each line being supported on a pair of strong lattice girders, and these were laterally stiffened by single diagonal bracings reaching from side to side. The piers at Queensferry and on Fife were very nearly in the same position as those of the present bridge, and there were two approach viaducts to reach the high ground upon either side. The bridge was to have been constructed entirely of steel.

Offices and workshops – which are now standing – were built at Queensferry, and extensive brickworks near Inverkeithing laid out and started. A brick pier – one of eight, which were to form the base of the great Inchgarvie tower – was built at the extreme north-west corner, after a foundation stone had been laid with great ceremony. But the collapse of the ill-fated Tay Bridge in December, 1879, stopped the further progress of the work, and the investigations into the causes of that disaster, and the disclosures made, shook the public confidence in Sir Thomas Bouch's design, and rendered a thorough reconsideration of the whole subject necessary. As a first result of this, the suspension bridge was abandoned, and the four railway companies above named instructed their consulting engineers – Messrs. Barlow, Harrison, and Fowler – to meet and consider the feasibility of building a bridge for railway

purposes across the Forth, and assuming the feasibility to be proved, to decide what description of bridge it would be most desirable to adopt. It was fairly well known how many types of bridge there were to select from for such a site; these were (1) Mr Bouch's original design; (2) three forms of suspension bridges with stiffening guides and braced chains; and (3) a cantilever bridge. The inquiry was most comprehensive. It embraced not only bridges as set forth, but also tunnels, and both of these for different sites.

With regard to tunnels, it was considered that the great depth of water in the two main channels – above 200 ft – and the high ground upon both shores, would necessitate very steep gradients and long approaches – making the tunnel many miles long, irrespective of the uncertainty of the nature of the ground through which the tunnel would have to be cut.

All things considered, the most suitable site for a bridge was held to be that at Queensferry; and, owing to the great depth of water and the nature of the bottom of the estuary, it was not considered expedient to construct a bridge with shorter spans than those which are indicated by the natural configuration of the ground.

The original design for a continuous girder bridge – on the cantilever and central girder principle which had been submitted by Messrs. Fowler and Baker – was in some particulars modified to suit the conflicting views of the other consulting engineers, and was then submitted to the directors in May, 1881. After consultation with the officers of the Board of Trade, this design was finally adopted, and Messrs. Fowler and Baker were appointed engineers to carry it into execution.

In July 1882 an Act of Parliament was obtained, authorising the construction of the bridge, and sanctioning

North British Railway Co. engine No. 661, outside Hawick Station, Roxburghshire, 1891.

the new financial arrangement by which the capital of the Forth Bridge Company was guaranteed with interest at 4 per cent per annum, each of the four contracting railway companies undertaking to find its share of the capital expenditure and pay its share of the interest. It is also agreed that the North British Railway Company will maintain the permanent way on the bridge, and conduct and manage all traffic, while the Forth Bridge Company undertakes to keep the structure generally in repair and good order.

Wilhelm Westhofen, *The Forth Bridge* (1890)

REMINISCENCES OF RAILWAYS

Not long after the opening of the North British line to Dolphinton, I spent a day at the southern end of the Pentland Hills, and in the evening, making my way to the village, found the train with its engine attached. The station was as solitary as a churchyard. After I had taken my seat in one of the carriages, the guard appeared from some doorway in the station, and I heard the engine-driver shout out to him, 'Weel, Jock, hae ye got your passenger in?'

The opening of a railway through some of these lonely upland regions was a momentous event in their history. Up till then many districts which possessed roads were not traversed by any public coach nor by many private carriages, while in other parishes, where roads either did not exist or were extremely bad and unfit for wheeled traffic, the sight of a swiftly moving train was one that drew the people from far

and near. Some time, however, had to elapse before the country-folk could accustom themselves to the rapidity and (comparative) punctuality of railroad travelling. When the old horse-tramways ran, it was a common occurrence for a tram to be stopped in order to pick up a passenger, or to let one down by the roadside, and it is said that this easy-going practice used to be repeated now and then in the early days of branch railways. An old lady from Culter parish, who came down to the railway not long after it was opened, arrived at the station just as the train had started. When told that she was too late, for the train had already gone beyond the station, she exclaimed, 'Dod, I maun rin then,' and proceeded at her highest speed along the platform, while the station-master shouted after her to stop. She was indignant that he would not whistle for the train to halt or come back for her.

Railway construction in the Highlands came later than it did in the Lowlands, and entered among another race of people with different habits from those of their southern fellow-countrymen. The natural disposition of an ordinary Highlander would not often lead him to choose the hard life of a navvy, and volunteer to aid in the heavy work of railway construction. The following anecdote illustrates a racial characteristic which probably could not have been met with in the Lowlands. During the formation of one of the lines of railway through the Highlands a man came to the contractor and asked for a job at the works, when the following conversation took place:

'Well, Donald, you've come for work, have you? and what can you do?'

''Deed, I can do onything.'

'Well, there's some spade and barrow work going on; you can begin on that.'

'Ach, but I wadna just like to be workin' wi' a spade and a wheelbarrow.'

'O, would you not? Then yonder's some rock that needs to be broken away. Can you wield a pick?'

'I wass never usin' a pick, whatefer.'

'Well, my man, I don't know anything I can give you to do.'

So Donald went away crestfallen. But being of an observing turn of mind, he walked along the rails, noting the work of each gang of labourers, until he came to a signal-box, wherein he saw a man seated, who came out now and then, waved a flag, and then resumed his seat. This appeared to Donald to be an occupation entirely after his own heart. He made enquiry of the man, ascertained his hours and his rate of pay, and returned to the contractor, who, when he saw him, good-naturedly asked:

'What, back again, Donald? Have you found out what you can do?'

''Deed, I have, sir. I would just like to get auchteen shullins a week, and to do that' – holding out his arm and gently waving the stick he had in his hand.

Sir Archibald Geikie

THOUGHTS ON MOTOR CARS

In January 1901 news came that Queen Victoria had passed away. For sixty-three years she had reigned over us, and few could remember a Britain without her. All realized that a glorious era had come to an end, and a new one started. Proof of this was not long in coming, as in June of that year Mr Elliot of Clifton Park arrived in a motor car and drove through the village. Most people had heard of this new invention, but few had actually seen a horseless carriage. The village turned out in mass to see this strange, noisy, and somewhat smelly vehicle. Not long after this Mr N. Ritchie of The Holmes bought a car, and thus became the first owner in St Boswells.

William Wilson, motor trader, St Andrews, sports his latest purchase at the turn of the century. Many dealers enthusiastically made the change from horse-drawn vehicles to motor cars.

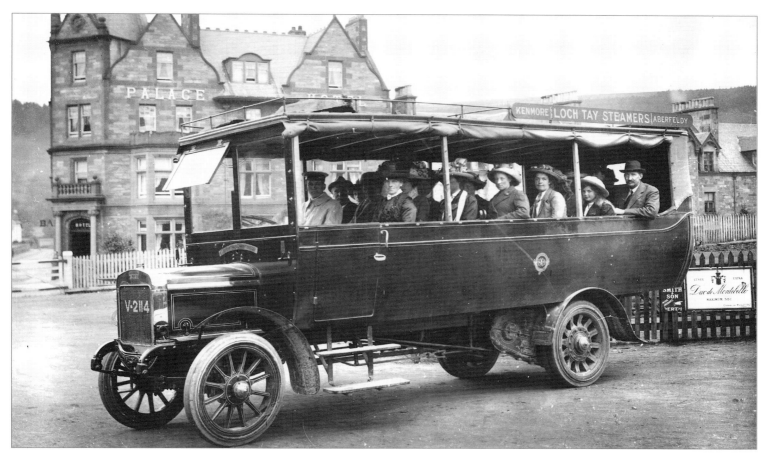

The Lanarkshire-registered Aberfeldy–Kenmore charabanc picking up passengers at Aberfeldy Station by the Palace Hotel. The first motor bus service began in Edinburgh in 1898. The railway companies were also pioneers of motor bus services.

The motor car was at first received with little enthusiasm by most people. Horses were prone to shy at them or sometimes to bolt. It was therefore customary for the driver to get out of his vehicle when he saw a motor approaching and hold his horse's head until the danger had passed. Even today this hazard is not entirely forgotten, and advertisements for the sale of horses often end with 'Quiet in traffic'. Though this is rather unjust, as horses and animals seem to have adapted themselves to motors rather better than human beings, if we are to judge by the number of casualties annually happening on our roads.

Farmers particularly disliked motors, as they were accustomed to drive their flocks and herds on the roads. The sudden appearance of a motor often left the unfortunate attendant and his dog to collect the scattered cattle and also to suffer the anger of proprietors on whose land the terrified animals had taken refuge. The old-fashioned roads of those days were not made for fast-moving traffic. In dry weather it stirred up clouds of dust, and in wet spattered pedestrians with mud. . . .

It would seem that the success of garages in the dawn of motoring depended more on the frequent repairs needed by individual cars than on the number present in [a] village. About the same time a car hire business started, the driver charging 1s 6d a mile. Considering the low price of petrol at that time, large profits must have been made.

Lt-Col. Frederick G. Peake, *Change at St Boswells* (1961)

A CARTER'S MEMORIES

Mine was a typical country family, which came into Dundee to get work in the jute mills. Like many agricultural labourers and crofters driven by economic necessity off the land, the only adaptable skills of my father and brothers were with horses. So they became town carters. When my Dad went out carting, I was about 10 or 12; that would be about 1887 or 1889. He went out at 5 a.m. and I never saw him back till 8 at night. My brother Bill was 'on the beef'; he was a keen union lad.

The carters were very close to the dockers and railway workers in Dundee, because they would always be driving loads to one or other, even if they weren't employed by one of the three companies of railway cartage contractors.

Jute lorries with loads of two hundred-weight bales had two horses; later a motor truck could take four times as much. From Cox's jute mill two-horse and one-horse lorries went to the docks; the journey was to fill up with jute, and it was a mile and a half trip. When they took a big boiler out of Dundee it meant two dozen horses – impressive sight.

I liked polishing the harness for them. Amongst my early recollections were the decorated horse parade shows, in aid of the hospital or Life Boats. The first holiday I ever had was when I went to Leith with brother Bill, who was a grooming expert. I helped him; and he took first prize.

Bob Steward (*c.* 1950)

THE CARTERS' LIFE

The custom was for a carter to be allotted by the employers a number of rakes, or journeys, when he started from the stables at 5.30 a.m. He went on working until these were completed, no matter what the conditions. This could mean waiting hours at dock gates or railhead for his turn to be unloaded. Traffic blocks, the closing of bridges and quays — none of this was taken into account. Even when he had finished his last rake, he had to bring his horse back to stables and see to it before he plodded his own way home, just as he had to groom his horse next morning before the weary day began. Not only did he work six days in the week, but every Sunday he had to come into the stables, without pay, to attend to the animals, on penalty of a fine if he did not do so. The earliest demand, as in the case of the old National Scottish Horsemen's Union in 1891, was not to reduce the hours, but to reduce the number of rakes, or to be paid overtime for rakes over and above a certain number.

There were three main classes of workers. The first group were the men who did the cartage work in connection with the railways. Some worked directly for the railway companies from company stables, such as the 'Caledonian men' or the 'Terminus men' in Glasgow. The rest were employed by the three large firms of railway cartage contractors, who specialized in this work all over Scotland and were known as the 'Railway contractors'. Next, there were the Corporation men, employed by the local authorities, ranging from cleansing to passenger transport. There was also a vast number of haulage contractors, from small firms to large ones, known as the 'general contractors', some of whom specialized, for example in coal, flour, timber, brewery work, and jute. A section which became of increasing importance comprised the delivery services of the co-operative societies, from bakery and milk vans to hearses. At this time, wages varied from 19*s* to 21*s* a week for the railway carters, with certain extras; 26*s* for Corporation carters; from 17*s* to 25*s* for the general contractors' men; and for the co-operative societies' men between 24*s* and 27*s*.

Angela Tuckett, *The Scottish Carter* (1967)

Two Berwickshire carters pose for John Wood in 1910. Before the development of motor transportation Scotland's goods were moved about the country by rail and a network of thousands of carters and their teams of horses.

Chapter 8

ROMANCING THE SEA

The years just before the First World War saw a huge rise in interest in Scotland in matters maritime, fuelled by the popular press which presented warships as advanced products of modern technology. There was a development too, of the peaceful uses of Scots maritime engineering and a public enthusiasm for vessels taking part in the Blue Riband of the Atlantic – an award for the fastest seaborne crossing of the Atlantic – first awarded in 1838.

Scotland's ports formed a link for her iron, coal, whisky and minerals industries with the international markets. And the country's shipyards, on the Clyde in particular, were patronised by both the British Admiralty and the great steamship companies. Scotland was to be the cockpit for the development of the large passenger liner. The triple-screw Virginian was one such. Built at Glasgow in 1904 by Alexander Stephen & Sons Ltd for the Allan Line, the liner headed a long list of marine engineering triumphs that were to include Cunarders like the Carmania (1905), of John Brown's shipyards and the Lusitania (1907), whose second voyage broke the existing transatlantic record.

Some of the world's first warships came from Scotland's shipyards, with the battleship Tiger and the battle-cruisers Inflexible and Repulse slipping out of John Brown's yards. Clydeside gave employment to some eighty thousand men and boys, who often enjoyed holiday trips 'doon the watter' in pleasure steamers they had constructed. Of these the King Edward (1901) was favourite, on the route from Craigendoran to Campbeltown.

In July the river was at its busiest when the yacht clubs organised their 'Clyde Fortnight' of regattas and races. All the folk in coastal Dumbartonshire and Renfrewshire became ardent cutter-yacht spotters, each identifying vessels that perhaps a member of their families had helped to build. Company rivalry was keen; thus the men from D.W. Henderson's yards at Meadowside, Patrick, glowed with pride when the Prince of Wales's 1893 yacht Britannia winged its way to victory in the Royal Largs and Royal Northern Club races. Henderson's men were ecstatic when the same year the yacht Valkyrie II, which they had built for the Earl of Dunraven and Mount-Earl, won the prize of the Royal West of Scotland Club.

Not only did the construction of seagoing vessels provide a livelihood for thousands of Scots, the fruits of the sea sustained thousands more. Scots fishermen in their sailing smacks and steam-trawlers fished for herring which were cured and exported to such places as Germany and the Baltic. There were three 'seasons' in the Scots herring year: January to March the fishermen sailed north to Wick and Stornoway or fished the Firth of Forth; April to September saw them off the east coast, Orkney and Shetland, while in October to November they sailed off to the waters off Yarmouth and Lowestoft. They were followed by an army of highly skilled fisher-lasses who gutted the caught fish on the quays. These girls worked an eighteen-hour day and were paid in gold sovereigns. Hard was the work for all connected with the sea but a strong relationship was sustained.

The training ship TTS Mars being towed to her berth off Newport-on-Tay, Fife. The 80-gun warship was built for the Royal Navy in 1848. She was refitted as an industrial training ship after the Crimean War and brought to the Tay in 1869. She was the home for 400 boys aged 12–16 who were given basic training in seamanship. The vessel was broken up in 1929.

The 20,000 ton battleship HMS Colossus *laid down by Scotts of Greenock in 1909. She was the first of the Dreadnought Class built on the Clyde and entered the 2nd Division Home Fleet to become flagship of Admiral Gaunt at the Battle of Jutland, 1916.*

PIONEER SHIPBUILDERS

The maintenance of an industry for two hundred years by one family, in the direct line of succession and in one locality, is almost unique in the history of western manufactures. Such a record indicates the maintenance of a high standard of workmanship as well as integrity and business capacity; because time is the most important factor in proving efficiency and in establishing credit for durability of work, without which no reputation can be retained for a long period.

The Scotts began the building of ships in Greenock in 1711. Today, their descendants of the sixth generation worthily maintain the high traditions of the intervening years. To give an adequate impression of the service rendered by the firm to the science of marine construction we should require to review in detail the successive steps: firstly, in the perfection of the sailing ship, from the sloops and the brigantines of the eighteenth century, to such beautiful clippers as Scotts' *Lord of the Isles*, which in 1856 made the record voyage from China, and did much to wrest from the Americans the 'blue ribbon' of the ocean; secondly, in the development of the merchant steamship from its inception early in the nineteenth century to the leviathans of today; and, thirdly, in the increase in fighting efficiency of all types of warships, from the submarine – the first vessel of which class fitted with steam turbine machinery was built by

them for the British Navy, to the modern super-Dreadnought, of which they contributed examples to the British fleet which won a glorious victory in the great European war of 1914–1918.

In successive epochs in the history of naval architecture the Scotts have played a creditable part, and to some of the more important improvements initiated or advanced by the firm reference will be made in our brief survey of the work done during the past two centuries. Unfortunately, some years ago, most of the old-time records were destroyed by a fire at the shipyard, so that our review of the early work is largely from contemporary publications, and is unavoidably incomplete.

The beginnings were small, for Scotland had not yet attained to industrial importance, and had little oversea commerce. The first trans-Atlantic voyage by a Clyde ship was made in 1686, when a Greenock-built vessel was employed on a special mission to carry twenty-two persons transported to Carolina for attending conventicles and 'being disaffected to Government'. American ships were most numerous on the western seas. The East India Company had a monopoly of the eastern seas, so far as Britain was concerned, and preferred to build their ships in India, although many were constructed on the south coast of England. This monopoly checked progress.

Two Centuries of Shipbuilding by the Scotts at Greenock (1920)

FAMOUS YARDS, FAMOUS SHIPS

Barclay, Curle & Co.

1818   John Barclay begins shipbuilding at Stobcross Pool.
1855   Moves to Whiteinch.
1870   Specialises in cargo-passenger vessels.
1892   Builds steam yacht *Capercailzie*.
1907   Builds *City of Paris* for City Line.

John Brown Shipbuilding & Engineering Co.

1847   Firm begins as marine engineers.
1852   Launches Cunard paddle-steamer *Jackal*.
1913   Builds RMS *Aquitania* for Cunard.

Charles Connell & Co.

1861   Yard founded at Scotstoun.
       Builds tea clippers.
1883   Builds the Inman Line *City of Chicago*.

William Denny & Bros

1845   Dumbarton yard founded. First vessel PS *Loch Lomond*.
1901   Turbine passenger steamer *King Edward*.

Lithgows

1874   Takes over bankrupt yard.
1878   Builds *Falls of Clyde*.
1905   *River Clyde*, converted troop landing craft for Gallipoli.

Fairfield Shipbuilding & Engineering

1880   *Livadia* yacht built for Russian Czar.
1905   *Empress of Britain* for Canadian Pacific Steamship Co.

Robert Napier & Sons

1821   Marine engineers.
1855   *Persia*, first iron mail ship for Cunard.
1861   *China*, first screw-driven mail ship.
1900   Bought out by William Beardmore & Sons.

Scotts of Greenock

1711   Founded.
1819   *Robert Bruce*, the first steamer to trade between the Clyde and Liverpool.
1912   Builds *S1*, the first submarine to be launched in Scotland.
1913   *Transylvania*, Anchor Line, largest vessel to have been built on lower Clyde.

William Simons & Co.

1810   Commences, Greenock.
1851   *William Connal*, first vessel fitted with wire rigging.

Alexander Stephen & Sons

1750   Shipbuilders, Burghead, Morayshire.
1854   Iron ships in Clyde, build their first steamship *William McCormick*.
1867   *Abeona*, fastest clipper in the Allan Line's North Atlantic fleet.

Warships fitting out at Cartsburn dockyard, east of Greenock, Renfrewshire. The special 690 ft basin opened out into the Clyde and a feature of the yard was the 120 ton electric crane.

The office building and entrance to Fairfield Shipbuilding and Engineering Works, 1909. Benefitting from pioneer advances in steel technology, Scotland easily maintained her shipbuilding supremacy before 1914. Clydeside builders John Brown (who acquired the controlling interest in Harland & Wolff in 1906) remained the biggest builders of passenger vessels.

THE 'INDOMITABLE' CLASS

The 'Indomitable' type, of which three have been constructed, resembles a battleship more closely than any other cruiser yet built. Indeed they are the most remarkable cruisers yet constructed, and indicate the present-day conception of the cruisers of the immediate future. The line of demarcation of the duties, as well as of the design, of battleship and cruiser were formerly clearly defined. The one was designed for taking part in the line of battle; the other as primarily a commerce protector or scout, analogous to the frigate of former times.

THE TURBINE STEAMER *VIPER*

Turning now to passenger steamers for coastal service, reference may first be made to the Glasgow and Belfast trade, upon which runs one of the most successful turbine steamers of the day – the *Viper*. This vessel was constructed at the Fairfield Works for Messrs G. and J. Burns, Limited, who have been associated with the Clyde and Belfast trade since 1825 and first undertook the royal mail nightly service in 1849. The daylight service was commenced in 1889 with the

Cobra, built at Fairfield in that year. Her length is 265 ft. The succeeding vessel, the *Adder*, built in the following year, is 280 ft long; and the *Viper*, constructed in 1906, is 315 ft in length, and of 1710 tons – exactly double the tonnage of the first vessel for the daylight service. There is accommodation for 1700 passengers. With a total load of 245 tons, and a draught of 11 ft 6 in, the vessel maintained a speed of over 22 knots on her official trials, the contract speed being 21 knots.

On service the *Viper* makes the voyage at 21½ knots, and is a very popular vessel.

The Fairfield Shipbuilding and Engineering Works (1909)

SINKING OF THE *TITANIC*

The *Titanic* was launched at the Belfast shipyards of Harland and Wolff on 31st May, 1911. She was eleven storeys high and a sixth of a mile long and was claimed to be the largest and safest vessel afloat. A passenger embarking at Southampton for her maiden voyage asked one of the deck hands, 'Is this ship really unsinkable?' 'Yes, lady,' he said, 'God himself could not sink this ship.'

The armoured 20,125 ton battlecruiser HMS Indomitable *was launched in 1907 by Fairfield Shipbuilding and served in the Dardanelles blockade and took part in the Battle of Jutland.*

The turbine steamer Viper *was built by Fairfield Shipbuilding for the Clyde–Belfast Mail Service. The vessel undertook the first daylight sailings from Greenock to Belfast in 1890.*

Scots emigrants aboard the 'Titanic hero' SS Carpathia, 1912. The 13,603 ton vessel was completed by Swan Hunter in 1903 for the busy transatlantic emigrant traffic. She was designed to carry 200 second-class and 1,500 steerage passengers; her first-class accommodation was upgraded in 1905.

The Cunard liner Carpathia, under Captain Arthur Henry Rostron, answered the Titanic's distress call on 4 April 1912. The vessel rescued 705 of the stricken vessel's passengers and conveyed them to New York. Carpathia was hit by a torpedo during the First World War and sank in 1918.

Mr C.H. Stengel, a first-class passenger, said that when the *Titanic* struck the iceberg the impact was terrific, and great blocks of ice were thrown on the deck, killing a number of people. The stern of the vessel rose in the air, and people ran shrieking from their berths below. Women and children, some of the former naturally hysterical, having been rapidly separated from husbands, brothers and fathers, were quickly placed in boats by the sailors, who like their officers, it was stated, were heard by some survivors to threaten men that they would shoot if male passengers attempted to get in the boats ahead of the women. Indeed, it was said that shots were actually heard. Mr Stengel added that a number of men threw themselves into the sea when they saw that there was no chance of their reaching the boats. 'How they died,' he observed, 'I do not know.' He dropped overboard, caught hold of the gunwhale of a boat, and was pulled in because there were not enough sailors to handle her. In some of the boats women were shrieking for their husbands; others were weeping, but many bravely took a turn at the oars.

A vast fortune in personal possessions was left behind in the first-class cabins of the *Titanic*. Mrs Dickinson Bishop abandoned all her jewellery estimated to be worth $11,000 and Major Arthur Peuchen decided against taking a tin box which contained $200,000 in bonds and $100,000 preferred stock.

The *Titanic* was the last ship to use the distress call CQD ('come quick danger'). When the Captain realized that his two wireless operators were unable to raise help, he ordered them to try the latest code. Thus the *Titanic* was the first vessel to use the distress call SOS ('save our souls').

The Times

The *Titanic* carried 1316 passengers and crew of 891. Over 1500 lives were lost on the night of the 15 April 1912. More than half the first-class passengers were saved, but only 23 per cent of the third-class passengers were rescued.

'I only realised the situation was serious when I saw a working-class passenger on the first-class deck' (*Titanic* survivor).

Daily Herald, 22 April 1912

TITANIC AND CARPATHIA

The great 'Titanic' sped her way
Across the Atlantic all well found,
Her passengers were blythe and gay –
For many there were homeward bound.

Her crew, the pick of able men,
The Captain trusted through long years,
All ready to do duty when
The call came ringing on their ears.

'A ship unsinkable' 'twas said!
But what can cope with Nature's powers
Man's skill oft in the dust is laid
And over all 'th' Almighty towers'.

Oh happy were the ones on board,
No danger in the distance loomed
Yet overhead there hung the sword
Of cruel fate: 'the ship was doomed'.

The night was clear, the stars were out,
Those Sentinels of Heaven above
Which shine for aye to quell all doubt
That 'He who rules the waves' is love.

'A treach'rous iceberg' barred her way,
The vessel struck as 'twere a rock;
The helm was turned without delay,
'Too late': some felt the fatal shock.

A wireless message flashed through space,
Caught by 'Carpathia'; on she sped!
Swift to the rescue, 'noble race!
To save souls from a watery bed.'

The word was given 'put out the boats!'
And 'women, children, pass along';
There's hope yet, while the vessel floats,
The weak went first, for love was strong.

Brave women linked to husbands dear,
Resolved to stay with them and die
'True heroines' they still appear,
Death could not snap love's sacred tie.

In fancy we may try to scan
The engineers at work below,
Who nobly perished to a man,
From duty's post they would not go.

The bandsmen playing at their post
The hymn 'Nearer my God to Thee',
While many ere death's bar was cross'd
The Heav'nly Pilot's face would see.

The fatal moment came at last,
When plunging down into the deep
The mighty vessel sinking fast
Drew precious souls to their last sleep.

'Your glorious deeds, true noble souls,
Will live, and men will speak of them
While o'er you th' Atlantic rolls
And plays a constant requiem.'

John E. Melvin, *Alloa Advertiser,* 'Poetical Tributes on the Loss of the RMS Titanic', ed. Charles F. Forshaw (1912)

THE LIFE OF A FISHER-LASSIE

The Scottish fisher-girls see more of the British Isles than the average British woman. It happens in this way. Herrings are to be found at various seasons in different waters. Schools of herrings lodge within the Firth of Forth from January until March, while they are to be found in the vicinity of the North-Eastern Coast of England from April until June; then from July until September they visit the waters of the German Ocean in the vicinity of Eyemouth. The months of October to December see shoals of herrings in the south, near to Yarmouth and Lowestoft. This outline of the movements of the herring, of course, is localised, and is given here simply in order to show dwellers in the country and inland towns that the herring is a seasonable fish. The great fishing grounds have their centres – Scalloway in the Shetlands, and Stornoway in the Hebrides; Thurso, Fraserburgh, Anstruther, Eyemouth, Lowestoft, and Yarmouth. To these centres do the fishing fleets carry their catches.

Women workers are needed to receive the herrings, and for the purposes of gutting and packing and smoking them. The girls are engaged ahead for the various seasons. It is necessary, therefore, that they should 'travel the herring', *i.e.*, follow the fishing fleet. As there is no employment in Eyemouth other than the fishing industry, probably a hundred or so of our young women are engaged in this work at the various fishing centres all the year round.

The quantities of herrings landed daily from the various fleets are so large that a fresh market could not use the constant supply, so that shiploads of pickled herrings are despatched to Continental ports, such as Hamburg, Stettin and other Baltic towns. The consignment of herrings to these foreign places necessitates curing. This is where woman's work comes in.

Upon landing, the herrings are immediately salted as they lie in great oblong tubs or tanks. From these tubs or tanks they are taken and packed for shipment. In this connection the women work in sets of three, and they are paid at the rate of 1*s* a barrel, if engaged for piece-work; or the terms may be 8*s* a week, herrings or no herrings, and 6*d* or 8*d* for every barrel packed. It takes a quick eye and a smart hand to engage in the work of selecting. The bad is separated from the good, the large from the small. When you think that there are about 850 herrings in every barrel of 'selected' you will wonder that the girls are able to make a living. But this they do, and their incomes, when herrings are plentiful, are by no means small, for experience teaches them to go at their work with such effort that mind and hand are in constant action.

Women from the workforce of Scotts of Greenock pictured in 1916. The war gave a great boost to work opportunities for women as the men went off to war. The number of women in employment in Scotland increased by one million and those working in munitions and war materials could earn more than £2 per week.

A Firth of Forth paddle-steamer at anchor at Largo Pier, c. 1910. The railway viaduct, over which trains first ran in 1856 and which linked Fife locations with the Newhaven ferry, is seen in the background.

A flash of the eye marks out the various qualities, and, as soon as the impression is conveyed to the brain, the hand picks out the herring. It is dexterously accomplished, and so well up to their work are the fisher-girls that they can pick out and pack, pickling at the same time with coarse salt, thirty-three barrels per set of three girls per day. As they are paid at the rate of 1s a barrel, each girl can make as much as 11s in a single day. . . .

But to prevent putrefaction the fish must be 'cured' immediately upon arrival, and this often means that the girls have to stand on their feet for as many as fourteen hours at a stretch, with breaks of a few minutes for meals. And this not in a warm room, but in the open, exposed to wind and rain, hail and snow. Sometimes the girls will be working among ice, with hands and feet numb, and the cold gripping at their hearts until they fall into a faint. This is a common experience of the fisher-girls.

For her there is no Factory Act, if she works on the quay; and whether on a quay or in a shed, she does not have the sitting accommodation provided by Act of Parliament for shop-girls.

For a protection from the severe weather the girls wear Wellington boots, and their lower limbs are protected by an oilskin skirt. Their arms must always be free, so that this prevents them wearing oilskin jackets. Illnesses are very common amongst the girls, especially during trying weather. Many break down in health. In certain parts, too, they have no one to look after their cooking arrangements. One of their number (those who live in the same room) is appointed to leave off work a half-hour or so before meal time to prepare their food. But when business is brisk (as time means money, and as inclination is not easy to turn in the way of domestic duty after hours of hard work on the quay), it is not surprising to know that the most easily prepared meal is often chosen. Preserved meats and tea have a good deal to do with the illnesses common to fisher-girls. There are many victims to indigestion and anaemia. . . .

Montrose fisherwomen packing herring, c. 1880. The herring were packed into barrels after being gutted and salted, and were examined by the Fishery Officer who branded the barrels and stencilled them for export with a crown mark.

The ocean-going yacht Erin *was built in 1896 and purchased by Sir Thomas Lipton (1850–1931). Thomas Johnstone Lipton, the Scots businessman and philanthropist, was born in Glasgow of Irish parents. He began work as an errand boy and in 1865 he went to America where he worked on a tobacco plantation and in a grocer's shop. He returned to Glasgow in 1870 and opened his first grocery store at Finnieston. This developed into the grocery empire which made him a millionaire by the time he was thirty. Lipton was always a keen yachtsman and in 1899 he made his first challenge for the America's Cup. This sailing race is held periodically off Newport, Rhode Island, and in it US yachts are challenged for a cup won by* USS America *off the Isle of Wight in 1851. Scotland's great tea baron exemplified Scotland's 'rags to riches' stories, and he embodied the benefits to be accrued from the primary Victorian virtues of thrift and hard work.*

Another trouble which afflicts these hard-worked girls is knife-wounds. A sharp knife is used in the processes of curing and gutting. In the former every herring has the gills removed from it, while in the latter, which is necessary for the purposes of kippering, the herring is opened up and all internal organs are removed. This is called simply 'gutting'. The speed of the knife is responsible for the frequency of wounded hands. There is another cause, however, and that is the hardness of the herring's jaws. To protect the thumb while in the act of cutting out the gills, it is wrapped with a piece of cotton. It is matter for notice that so many of the girls have wounded hands. . . .

What are the prospects of the fisher-girl? As a rule, she marries a fisherman. No other woman could do so well as the helpmeet of a fisherman. His wife must be conversant with he 'gear', she must be able to 'bait' nets – in other words, mend the torn meshes – or she'll fail as a wife. The fisher-girl makes the best fisherman's wife. Although intermarriage is very common in fishing villages, occasionally, owing to the travelling system, men and women from different parts are thrown in each other's way, with the inevitable result in many cases. Love enriches the song of the fisher-girl as she deftly uses the gut-knife, for she knows that if the 'drave', or the season's work, be successful, her fisher-lad will have the banns proclaimed immediately he has a fair amount of 'siller' with which to marry.

Revd Daniel McIver, *An Old-Time Fishing Town: Eyemouth* (1906)

The naming ceremony of the first lifeboat at St Abbs, Berwickshire, 25 May 1911. The vessel was stationed at St Abbs after the shipwreck of the Alfred Eralsden *in 1907, a tragedy in which fourteen lives were lost.*

AN ANTICIPATORY HOLIDAY

THE most poignant pleasure of the holiday season is anticipation, and to realise that to the fullest one must begin to wrestle about May with the problem, 'Where to go.' Steamship companies must be despoiled of time-tables; courteous clerks must be seized by the throat, while they prattle about the Riviera, Paris, Egypt, and the Occident. The beginning of June decides that Belgium will be the land on which to descend, and you weigh the joys of Rotterdam and the Rhine with the giddy delights of Brussels and Ostend. Choosing the latter, the traveller reads up about the old-fashioned houses, the quaint people, Waterloo, mixed bathing, and the numerous other strange sights to be seen in the battlefield of Europe. And when his holiday comes he rushes to the railway station, buys a ticket, and is seen for the usual fortnight on the pier or the promenade at Rothesay.

The Bailie, 1903

CANAL TRAVEL

Much more leisurely was the transit on the Union Canal. The boats were comfortably fitted up and were drawn by a cavalcade of horses, urged forward by postboys. It was a novel and delightful sensation, which I can still recall, to see fields, trees, cottages, and hamlets flit past, as if they formed a vast moving panorama, while one seemed to be sitting absolutely still. For mere luxury of transportation, such canal-travel stands quite unrivalled. Among its drawbacks, however, are the long detentions at the locks. But as everything was new to me in my first expedition to the west, I remember enjoying these locks with the keenest pleasure, sometimes remaining in the boat, and feeling it slowly floated up or let down, sometimes walking along the margin and watching the rush of the water through the gradually opening sluices.

Both the stage-coaches and the passenger boats on the canal were disused after the opening of the Edinburgh and Glasgow Railway in the spring of 1842. A few weeks subsequent to the running of the first trains, the *Glasgow Courier* announced that 'the whole of the stage-coaches from Glasgow and Edinburgh are now off the road, with the exception of the six o'clock morning coach, which is kept running in consequence of its carrying the mail bags.'

Sir Archibald Geikie

THE YACHT WITH MANY ROLES

The *Aegusa* was designed and built in 1896 for a Sicilian nobleman, and was purchased later by Sir Thomas Lipton,

from the New York Herald.

SIR THOMAS LIPTON AND THE CUP.

This US cartoon published by The Bailie *in 1903 parodies Lipton's keenness to win the America's Cup. At various times between 1899 and 1930 Lipton made four unsuccessful attempts to win the prestigious cup.*

who re-christened her the *Erin.* One of the largest yachts of her time, she was 250 ft long, and of 1330 tons displacement. The four-cylinder balanced engines of 2500 indicated horse-power gave a sea speed of 15.6 knots. This yacht had an interesting history. Shortly after the outbreak of war Sir Thomas fitted her out as a hospital ship, and proceeded to the Near East on a mission to the Serbians. Later there was a reversion to the original name of *Aegusa* when the Admiralty took her over as an armed patrol steamer, there being already an *Erin* in the Navy. She did good work on our coasts until her career was ended by an enemy torpedo.

Fairfield Shipbuilding and Engineering

Ratings of the British Channel Fleet fall in at St Andrews harbour, c. 1910. Before the First World War the fleet regularly 'laid off' St Andrews Bay.

The launch of a battleship at Cartsburn Dockyard of Scotts of Greenock, Renfrewshire. Shipworkers and their families took great pride in the ships on which they had toiled, and followed the vessels' 'careers' with great interest.

Chapter 9

HEBRIDEAN MEMORIES

*T*oday they call them the Hebrides. To the ancient Scots Celts they were Innsegall ('Isles of the Foreigners'), and to the Vikings they were Sudreyar ('The Southern Isles'). No one knows the meaning of the word Hebrides – an undoubted mistranslation of Hebudes in old texts – but their position on the western edge of continental Europe leaves these Western Isles much as they were a hundred years ago, and a dozen or so decades before that.

Sited west of the Isle of Skye and west coast mainland Scotland, the Hebrides are made up of Barra and the Long Island chain from Harris and Lewis to North Uist, Benbecula and South Uist. Farmers have herded cattle and tilled the soil here from around 8000 BC and the islands bear the marks of the passage of such as Bronze Age development, Celtic Christianity and the Vikings.

The pursuit of a Celtic heritage, the islands' distinctive flower-lore and birdlife and the romance of the Outer Isles where mermaids were said to take mortal husbands, brought hundreds of Victorian travellers on the ferries from the industrial west of Scotland. Queen Victoria herself never visited the Outer Isles, although she did take a trip round the west coast of Scotland aboard the Royal Yacht Victoria and Albert in 1847; however, on 2 September 1902, Provost Anderson and the people of Stornoway welcomed King Edward VII and Queen Alexandra with great enthusiasm.

Such visitors, whether illustrious or unknown, found memories of a thousand years of Hebridean life set in oral traditions and the physical shape of the islands. They photographed and took notes of the traditional house types, the peat cutting and seaweed gathering and the sheep husbandry that had replaced, in part, the cattle farming of old. They were charmed by the typical Hebridean dwelling, the earth and clay black house, which served as both home and byre. And they marvelled at how kelp, called seaware in the Hebrides, had been used as a fertiliser from antiquity. The winter harvest of seaweed produced huge dumps along the coastline, and the drying walls of great historic interest were to be viewed all along the west coast.

The activity of the peat cutters, a tradition as old as seaweed gathering, necessitated great skill to slice and stack the peat in weatherproof piles by house and farm. Often old uncaptioned photographs of homesteads can be identified by the design of the peat stacks and the shape of the peats. Still to be found in use in the Hebrides one hundred years ago were the ancient relics of cultivation, from the footplough (caschrom) to the peat-cutter (treisgir), while houses were lit with oil lamps (cruisie) and milk was heated for nourishment in clay vessels (ballachan).

Yet it was a land of shrinking population. Epidemics, failed harvests, remoteness and the anachronistic modes of living all led to islands and communities being deserted. To this day the

A typical crofter's house outside Stornoway, Isle of Lewis, c. 1910. Other houses are seen in an advanced state of ruination by this date and peats are stacked to the right for winter fuel.

islanders retain an independence of spirit and a verve to preserve their way of life just as it was when the Victorians visited.

THE EVICTION

On one of our visits to North Uist we were much concerned at a glimpse of a little tragedy so characteristic that I cannot refrain from relating it. A poor woman, very old, very feeble, lived alone in a wretched hut, which was undoubtedly an eyesore to any orderly minded proprietor. On the other hand, to its solitary occupant it meant home, and the alternative was the poorhouse. Eviction seemed inevitable, and some kindly neighbours, we were told, offered to build her a decent shelter – she was otherwise provided for – if the morsel of land, enough for an average cowshed, could be granted for the short term of life which remained to her. But no, among the thousands of bare acres all around, there was no room for so valueless a life as hers. The time came – the photograph of the scene is in my possession – when her few belongings were turned out by the roadside, and she herself laid upon the miserable bedding which, with a wooden chest, a couple of chairs, a single cooking pot, a few bits of crockery, constituted her entire wealth. When we saw her next she was sitting, decently fed and clad it is true, the sole occupant of a vast dreary 'Female Ward'. 'And how did you get here?' we asked, and it is for the sake of her answer, so thoroughly characteristic of Highland speech and thought, that I have told the little story. Her eyes filled with tears, and for a minute she stroked my hand in silence. 'It was himself that did it,' she answered, pointing to the master of the poorhouse, himself an islander, who has since, as often before, served his country 'at the front'. 'It was himself that did it, and may the blessed angels carry him to heaven as gently as he carried me here that day.' There was no word of what she had lost, no reproach, no bitterness. To him from whom she had received kindness, she had nothing to give but prayer to the One who has 'constituted the services of angels and men in a wonderful order', a gift which brings blessing alike to 'him that gives and him that takes'.

A. Goodrich Freer, *Outer Isles* (1902)

COURTESY

I have seen those little groups, decent and orderly, sitting for hours together on the bare hillside, greeting one another and parting, with much hand-shaking, for indeed hand-shaking is a great institution in these friendly Islands, and I have seen no irreverence nor lack of sympathy in their conduct, nor in their presence there.

The gentle courtesy of the islander is no mere surface politeness to a stranger. The kindness of the people to each other and to the dumb creatures about them would be proof of this, if proof were wanting.

A. Goodrich Freer, *Outer Isles* (1902)

Crofter houses and stockyard at Carinish, North Uist, c. 1918. Stone, earth, peat and clay were the traditional building materials, with dry-stonewalling for the farmyards. In Gaelic the traditional island taigh-dubh ('black house') was made entirely of turf; while the 'white house' was built of stone.

KELP INDUSTRY

Kelp is made from two kinds of seaweed, the species called *fucus* which grows within tidal range and is cut from the rocks at low-water, and another variety, the *laminarias*, which is thrown up by the storms or other causes. When the drift-weed is seen coming in, those who live near the shore hoist a pole with a bundle of weed atop, and the cottars and poorer crofters hasten down to the shore, and men, women and children are occupied, whatever the weather, in removing the precious jetsam out of the reach of the sea, often working till the incoming tide is over the knees both of man and horse. It is then spread out on dry rocks – any admixture of sand being detrimental – until it putrifies and is then put into the kilns, each kiln holding about half a ton; a little dried straw being placed at the bottom. It is then set alight, and is allowed to burn for six or eight hours, being carefully watched the whole time, as, when the critical moment arrives, and the whole is reduced

Gathering kelp at South Uist. The ash produced when the seaweed was burned was used to make glass and chemicals. Also used as a fertiliser, seaweed was an economic mainstay of the islands of the 1880s.

to a fused mass, it is carefully raked, sprinkled with salt water, and broken up into convenient pieces. At this stage it looks like grey slag with streaks of white, blue, and brown, running through it. The kelp-rake is like a small spade, with a handle about seven feet long. Often, late into the summer night, one sees the fires of the kelp-burners twinkling along the shore in scores. The labour and watching required is immense, especially in collecting the drift-weed, which, for its present purpose, the distillation of iodine, is three or four times more valuable than the cut weed. The south-country people, and self-interested proprietors, who talk about 'the lazy Highlander' fail to realise that their work, fishing, kelp-making, crofting, is a war carried on at fearful odds with the elements, even in islands like Tyree, where, thanks to a kindly factor, they are not liable to be called off to the enforced estate labour which in certain districts frequently becomes imperative, immediately that the coming of the drift-weed is heard of. To produce one ton of kelp no less than twenty to twenty-two tons of seaweed are required, but such is the industry of these thrifty folk that even when the kelp has been as low as £2 10s a ton, a single family has been known to earn from £30 to £40 in a season.

The tangle gathering is a somewhat analogous industry, but is carried on in winter, and consists in collecting and drying the large shiny brown stalks thrown up by the tide, especially after a storm. These are gathered with a sort of narrow hay-fork, tossed ashore, and then collected in carts and stacked in a dry place. These stacks are of oblong shape, built to a certain height, and are paid for by the North British Chemical Company, at a given price per foot of length. The grieve who collects them, is provided with a long stick having an iron spike at the end, with which he pierces the pile at intervals, to ascertain that it contains no foreign matter, and that it is built fairly and on a level rock. The refuse, when cut away from the stalks, makes excellent manure for laying on the fields. A single storm will sometimes throw up enough tangle to keep a whole village occupied for two or three months.

A. Goodrich Freer, *Outer Isles* (1902)

LIVING CONDITIONS

The very existence of the island of South Uist is itself a tragedy which shames our civilization. Nowhere in our proud Empire is there a spot more desolate, grim, hopelessly poverty-stricken. It is a wilderness of rock and of standing water on which, in the summer, golden lichen and spreading water-lilies mock the ghastly secrets of starvation and disease that they conceal. The water is constantly utterly unfit for drinking purposes. There is not a tree on the island, and one wonders how the miserable cattle and sheep contrive to live on the scant grey herbage. The land of the poor is not enclosed; and to preserve the tiny crops from the hungry wandering cows and horses they have to be continually watched, and as half an acre of bere may be distributed over

The new post office, Stornoway, opened in 1908; a postal service (with office) had been established by 1756. The largest town in the old county of Ross-shire, Stornoway's harbour was a haven for the Scottish herring fleet.

five acres of bog and rock, the waste of human labour is considerable. The potatoes often rot in the wet ground, and I have seen the grain and hay lying out as late as October from the impossibility of getting it dried.

Excellent and abundant fresh-water trout there is, but that is not for the poor; nor the rabbits, nor the game, and even the sea-wrack, formerly a means of living, is now hardly worth the getting. Nevertheless, when the 'tangle' comes on the beach – provided the factor gives them leave to get it at all, which by no means necessarily follows – men, women and children crowd down with earliest daylight, and work on by moonlight or starlight, with the hideous intensity of starvation.

The houses of the poor, especially of the cottars, are inconceivably wretched. They are of undressed stone, piled together without mortar, and thatched with turf. Often they have no chimney, sometimes no window; the floor is a bog, and a few boxes, with a plank supported by stones for a seat, is all the furniture except the unwholesome shut-in beds. Cleanliness is impossible, with soot coating the roof overhead, wet mud for floor, and, except in the very rare fine days, chickens, and perhaps a sick sheep or even a cow or horse, for fellow-occupants.

A. Goodrich Freer

CHARACTER AND NATURE

It is not everyone who has been given the opportunity of studying the Highlander's character or the privilege of being able to appreciate it. The Highlander is infinitely patient, and he will minister to the requirements of the stranger as part of the respect which he owes to himself, but such courtesies are scattered, not elicited. It is in this faculty of patience that he differs from his nearest of kin in Ireland –

> The stranger came with iron hand
> And from our fathers reft the land,
> Where dwell we now? See rudely swell,
> Crag over crag, and fell o'er fell.
> Ask we this savage hill we tread
> For fattened steer or household bread?
> Ask we for flocks? These shingles dry
> And well the mountain might reply,
> To you as to your sires of yore
> Belong the target and claymore!

The Highlander's nature is too great for malice, too brave for petty revenges. If he is strong to suffer, he is strong also to endure.

He has the virtues and the failings of a child, or of the beasts who are his companions and friends. He is sensitive,

A popular cairt phostail *(postcard) of 1905 shows Mrs Macaulay's Westford Inn, Locheport, by Lochmaddy, the chief village of North Uist.*

Peat-cutting in the Outer Hebrides at the turn of the century. The traditional implement for the job was a tapering triangular wooden device with a footrest and horizontal cutting blade; it was called a caschrom *in Gaelic.*

easily hurt; his memory is tenacious of a slight or of an injustice; but he has lived hand-in-hand with Nature, and it is not only in his gift of second-sight, in his friendship with bird and beast, in his joy in the glamour of his Islands, but also in capacity for friendship, and in readiness to exchange sympathy, that he shows that his ear has been ever close to the beatings of her heart.

A. Goodrich Freer

PEAT AND THATCH

The peat-cutting is still done, if possible, by the men, who leave the peats to dry; but the burden of bringing them home too often falls upon the women, as the men are away most of the autumn. The peats are cut flat and big, not brick-shaped as on the mainland, and require a great deal of drying before they are fit for use.

There are separate names for the peats: *Barrad* is the top peat, *Gollad* the outside peat, *Treasad*, the third peat, *Siomad* the one most protected.

Much labour is spent over the thatch of the houses, which, if attended to from time to time, may last for forty years. The material mainly used in Uist is the bent-grass from the machair, but the people have to pay in labour for permission to cut it. The bent, when dried, is extremely tough, and is sometimes woven into mats, bags, and horse collars; one industrious man in Benbecula makes excellent chairs of it, of design and outline just such as one sometimes sees in old-fashioned houses as having come from India. Sometimes rushes are used, if permission can be obtained to cut them, more rarely heather, bracken, or the *Osmunda regalis*. The walls are built three or four feet thick, but are pointed with lime, sometimes packed with sand, as in Tyree.

A. Goodrich Freer

ILLICIT GOODS

It is said that there was formerly a good deal of illicit trade in South Uist, and that Dutch smugglers landed goods on the island, but whether for the benefit of families of the Clan Ranald or whether the goods were brought with the view of conveyance to the mainland does not appear.

The shebeen or unlicensed drinking-shops have also, technically, disappeared, though one in South Uist lingered on until but a few years ago, and naturally there is some evasion of the excise by the many foreign traders who visit Barra and

Lewis during the short fish-curing season. Only this year we heard of a melancholy scene when some of the fishermen of a certain island were deluded into buying a considerable quantity of Eau de Cologne. Under the impression it was some new variety of *uisge* (strong water), they adjourned to the hill one afternoon, when resting from a night of fishing, and proceeded to drink it. Then followed a fearful thirst which the men on a Scotch or English boat induced them to appease with beer, and the results, as may be imagined, were highly disastrous.

A. Goodrich Freer

ERISKAY FOLK

The export industry of Eriskay is confined to salt fish and eggs, of which latter nearly £200 worth are sent out yearly. The hens very quickly deteriorate in the cold and damp climate, and the strain has frequently to be renewed, or for table purposes they would be entirely useless. Something like £125 per annum is spent in Eriskay in tobacco, which, when on the sea during long dark nights, wet, cold, and often hungry, is almost a necessity for the men. As far as one can observe, they seem extraordinarily moderate in their smoking, using a very small pipe, which does not, to the merely female intelligence, look worth the trouble of lighting. None of the women smoke, and only one or two old ones take snuff.

The women are said to be exceptionally strong in child-birth, which, considering their distance from medical aid and from all conveniences of life, speaks well for their adaptation to environment; and moreover the rate of mortality is very low among young children. Of late years the influenza plague has sorely troubled both Eriskay and South Uist, but otherwise the islanders seem strong and healthy, and Father Allan tells us that when he first came to the island, there were three people over ninety years of age.

Before the days of the parcel post, before even such small conveniences as now reach South Uist could be imported into Eriskay, before even the small amount of cultivation now achieved was possible, one wonders how the people lived, and we were interested in learning from Father Allan various details about matters of diet. In old days cabbage and the curly green kail were freely grown in South Uist, but after the evictions the people had no ground even if they had had the heart to cultivate it, and they fell back largely on certain wild vegetables which before had been used only in

A postcard showing the congregation emerging from Eriskay church, south of South Uist, 1906. At this time the parish priest was Father Alan MacDonald. Eriskay is the small island where HRH Prince Charles Edward Stuart landed on 23 July 1745.

emergency. The root of the pretty little silver-weed which grows so freely all over the island, is called in Gaelic 'the seventh food that comes out of the ground'; and a man, still living, says that he remembers seeing a large trunkful stored for winter use in his grandfather's house. (In the islands there are no cupboards, and everything is kept in boxes, which they call 'trunks'). This was in Harris, where, he says, the land used to be divided among the people at ploughing time, so that each might have a fair share of the weed, which came off the ground when it was being tilled, otherwise the land was held and worked in common, and not in separate crofts. . . .

When Eriskay was first inhabited, separate spots in the island were marked off for certain families, for collecting wild spinach. It is still found where seaweed has been lying on the land, but is not eaten now, nor would be except under pressure of hunger. The goose-foot, wild mustard, and young nettles were also boiled as food. Then there were certain kinds of sea-weed: the dulse is still used, raw or boiled, also a seaweed which grows on the rocks called *Sloak*, which is boiled with butter, so too another called *Gruaigean*, probably identical with Iceland moss. A broad-leafed seaweed called *liathag*, which grows among the tangle, is edible when heated over the fire and rubbed in the hands. Another weed called cock's-comb, *feamainn chirein*, found on the rocks at half-tide, serves a variety of purposes. It is eaten raw by the cattle, and is given to them boiled as a useful cathartic. It is also made into poultices for man and beast, and boiled to give a lustre to home-made cloth.

When potatoes were a novelty and still scarce, they used to be brought into the house, and hung from the roof in bags made of bent grass. They were first introduced into Uist about 1743, and the old proprietors anxious for the good of their people, threatened them with eviction when they refused to plant them, wisely as it turned out, for in ten years the Islands were covered with them. They proved a most valuable addition to the barley, rye, and coarse oats hitherto grown, not only for their own merits as food, but because they could be grown where nothing else would prosper, on account of the hopelessly wet nature of the soil in a great many places.

A. Goodrich Freer

IMPLEMENTS

The oldest implement in the Islands, possibly one of the oldest in the world's history, is the *cas-chrom*, the crooked spade (literally, crooked foot). It is still in use in certain districts – we have noticed it in Skye and in Harris – and is said to be far more effective than the plough, besides being suitable in positions practically inaccessible for horse-labour, for many an island plot is too small for a plough to turn in.

The *cas-chrom* is extremely strong. The right foot is placed upon the side pin, and the head, which is about 2 ft 9 in long, jerked into the ground with the entire weight of the labourer, who rests upon the long shaft or handle which measures between 5 and 6 ft. He works from right to left, walking backwards. In Harris and other districts where cultivation is by means of 'lazy beds', already described, this instrument is almost indispensable. There are various modifications, notably the *cas dhireach*, as to which some verses are recited, said to be the spontaneous address of a Lochaber drover on first seeing an islander at work with the less orthodox implement:

> 'Tis not the right stick
> You have got in your fist,
> You have gone beyond your senses
> You will never be right while alive;
> Little tillage will you do
> With the ugly stick
> You cannot raise a crop
> That will keep alive a child,
> My darling is the crookie
> That comes up to meet me,
> When my foot is on the side spur,
> Heavily and kindly.
> It is not the right stick
> You have got in your fist.

Then there is the *ràcan*, or clod-breaker, so primitive but withal so useful an implement that one may suppose it to have been unaltered from the earliest days of tillage. It is primarily used as a mallet, and the teeth are only called into requisition on occasion.

The *trèisgar* and the *plèitheag* are used in cutting peats, and however primitive are admitted to be very effective for their purpose. The head is shod with iron, and the labourer cuts the peats the size intended at one push, while a second man casts them out on to the nearest plot of dry ground ready for drying and subsequent stacking.

A. Goodrich Freer

WOMEN CARDING AND SPINNING

The *bràth* (two stones revolving one upon another) is by some thought to be the oldest form of handmill in existence; the *cnotag* is a very simple instrument for bruising grain for immediate use, and consists of a solid piece of rock, often merely rough hewn, with a hollow for receiving the grain.

The women, too, have their special implements, the *cards* for combing or carding the raw wool into fleecy curls ready for spinning in the graceful *cuibhioll*, the low Highland wheel, which must always revolve *dessil*, sunward, which is used with a special grace – put away with the sign of the cross, and on Saturdays with the loosened band, that the powers of evil may not find it ready to their hand on the day of rest. Then there are the *crois-iarna* and the more uncommon *lianradh* for winding the wool into skeins, and the *mùdag*, a basket made of osiers to contain the ball of wool during manipulation and so keep it from the floor, which at best is sanded, but may be wet and muddy, for it consists of the native earth more or less hardened by use, sometimes with a rock cropping through, and affected, even in the best-regulated households, by the state of the weather.

A. Goodrich Freer

Pony transport at Lochboisdale, South Uist, 1908. Such transport was vital over the rough tracks of the island linking the crofters with the ferry ports. Baskets like that carried by the pony were made locally.

FLOWER-LORE

The natives have many traditions and stories about the flora of their islands. The St John's wort is called the armpit-flower of Columba (*achlasan Cholumcille*), and the story is that the saint, who had engaged a child to herd cattle for a day and a night, found him weeping as the evening fell, lest, in the darkness, the cattle should stray away and he be blamed. St Colum plucked this flower and put it under the child's arm, bidding him sleep in peace, for no harm could befall him with this for protection. Virtue still lingers about the plant, and its golden stars are loved by the children and brought home to protect the cattle from the Evil Eye.

The wild carrot is the finest fruit ever seen by the children of the Outer Isles, and they value it as other children do apples. As they seek it they recite a Gaelic verse:

> Honey underground
> Is the winter carrot
> Between St Andrew's Day and Christmas.

If one child has the luck to find a double or forked one, they all crowd round to rub their hands against it, four times, repeating:

> Lucky folk, lucky folk,
> The luck of big carrots be upon me,

and then all begin to seek in the fortunate spot.

The fishermen will not wear clothes dyed with the lichen or crottle found on the rocks, though it is largely used in some places for children's clothing and for wool for knitting. They say 'it comes from the rocks and will go back to the rocks'; indeed the Eriskay people will not use it at all, living, as they do, in a wild sea and surrounded by treacherous rocks. The use of it was caricatured by one of the bards:

> 'Tis not the indigo of Edinburgh
> That would be for clothing to these kites,
> But lichen gathered by finger nails
> Scratched off the rocks.

The burdock is the nearest thing to a twig or switch known familiarly to many islanders, so destitute are they of wood. The children have a story known as *Rann nam meacann*, which relates how a wren and his twelve children failed to uproot it. The dandelion is called *bearnan Brighide*, 'the notched plant of Brigid'.

A. Goodrich Freer

PHOTOGRAPHIC CREDITS
& TEXT SOURCES

ILLUSTRATIONS

The author is particularly grateful for help in tracing some of
the pictures herein to Mr & Mrs Robert Thomson of
Coldingham for the illustrations in the John Wood
Collection; to Miss Alexia Lindsay, Hon. Archivist of Fettes
College; to Mr Francis Thompson of the Isle of Lewis; Miss
Seonaid M. McDonald, assistant Archivist of the Bank of
Scotland; Miss Catherine Taylor of the Local Studies Dept,
City of Aberdeen Library Services; Mrs E.M. Shepherd,
Glasgow; and Mrs C.G.W. Roads, MVO, Lyon Clerk and
Keeper of Records, Court of the Lord Lyon. All the
photographs are herewith credited with grateful thanks:
St Andrews Research and Lecture Projects: i, ii, v, 4, 17, 19,
22, 23, 26, 27, 28, 31, 36, 37, 40, 41, 42, 43, 45, 51, 52, 56,
60, 61, 62, 63, 64, 67, 68, 69, 71, 74, 76, 82, 83, 84, 92, 93,
94, 95, 98, 100, 102; Jim Russell, Broughty Ferry, ii;
Alexander Brown Paterson MBE, iii, 3, 85, 91, 99; C.P.
Milligan, Dundee, iv; The Estate of the late Rt Hon. The
Lord Home of the Hirsel Kt, vii, 2, 44, 59, 60; Perth
Museum & Art Galleries, 35, 78; John Wood Collection, 1,
3, 6, 7, 8, 9, 38, 46, 73, 84, 90, 100; Angus District Libraries,
99; Blair Atholl Estates, 29, 42; The Baron and Baroness of
Earlshall, 59; Ettrick and Lauderdale District Museum
Service, 56; Wilton Lodge Museum, Hawick, 53, 56, 87;
D.W. Veitch, 55; Purves (Royal) Collection, 10, 11, 12, 13;
Glamis Castle Estates, 41; Sir Archibald Edmonstone, 14, 15;
The Rt Hon. The Earl of Mansfield and Mansfield, 43, 54;
The Bank of Scotland Archives, 49, 50, 52; Aberdeen City
Libraries, 53; The Rt Hon. Earl of Perth, 33, 66; G.
Normand, 23; S. Summers, 22, 89; J. Cameron, 30; Court of
the Lord Lyon, Edinburgh, 39; Old Gala Club, 35; Elizabeth
McIntosh, 70; H. Sim, 75; Fettes College, 79; Mrs M. Irvin,
85; Mrs E.M. Shepherd, 88, 96, 101; Francis Thompson,
103, 104, 105, 106, 107, 108, 110.

TEXT

The following source books are credited for quotes with
thanks to the copyright owners, their heirs and successors:
Sir Archibald Geikie, *Scottish Reminiscences*, Maclehose, 1904;
Margaret Ross, *Memoires of a Private Nurse*, McNaughton &
Sinclair, 1928; Theodore Fontane, *Jenseits des Tweed: Bilder
und Breife aus Schottland*, 1860 [Translated: Nymphinburger
Verlagshandlung, 1963]; Russell (Amos) Kirk, *St Andrews*,
Batsford, 1954; Robert Chambers, *Traditions of Edinburgh*,
W. & R. Chambers, 1824; James Taylor, *The Pictorial History
of Scotland*, Virtue, 1859; Lady Johnson-Ferguson, *Epitaphs*,
Thurnam, 1913; Sir John Fleming, *Looking Backwards for
Seventy Years*, AUP, 1922; W.R. Kermack, *Historical Geography
of Scotland*, Johnston, 1926; Lady Carrington, *Diary* (1878),
Bodleian Library; Susan Tweedsmuir, *The Lilac and The Rose*,
London, 1952; Maureen E. Montgomery, *Guilded Prostitution*,
1870–1914; Mabell, Countess of Airlie, *Thatched with Gold*,
Hutchinson, 1962; R. McNair Wilson, *Doctor's Progress*,
1932; George Cornwallis-West, *Edwardian Hey-Days*,
Putnam, 1930; D.H. Edwards, *Glimpses of Men and Manners*,
Brechin Advertiser, 1920; E.S. Turner, *What the Butler Saw*,
Joseph, 1962; John Buchan *John Macnab*, 1925; Lady Cynthia
Asquith, *The Child at Home*, Nisbet, 1923; Lady Dorothy
Nevill, *Under Five Reigns*, Methuen, 1914; Cosmo Gordon
Lang, [Private Papers]; Robert Ford, *Children's Rhymes*,
Gardner, 1908; James T.R. Ritchie, *The Singing Street*, Oliver
& Boyd, 1964; Wilhelm Westhofen, *The Forth Bridge*,
Engineering Magazine, 1890; Angela Tuckett, *The Scottish
Carter*, Allen & Unwin, 1967; Frederick G. Peake, *Change at
St Boswells*, Privately, 1961; *Two Centuries of Shipbuilding by the
Scotts at Greenock*, 1920; *The Fairfield Shipbuilding and
Engineering Works*, 1909; Charles E. Forshaw (Ed), *Poetical
Tributes on the Loss of the RMS Titanic*, Stock, 1912; Revd
Daniel Mc Iver, *An Old-Time Fishing Town: Eyemouth*.
Menzies, 1906; A. Goodrich-Freer, *Outer Isles*, Constable,
1902. Revd James D Mitchell, *Parish of Dull*, 1950.

INDEX